Last Man Standing

The Legendary Chi-Lites
Featuring Marshall Thompson
by Marshall Thompson

◊

Introduction and Additional Transcriptions
by Dane Ladwig

◊

Edited by Bonnie Classen

©2014
Anytime Enterprises, LLC.
Chicago, Illinois

Interior and Cover Design by: cyrusfictionproductions.com

All rights reserved. No part of this publication may be reproduced, stored in a retrieval system, in part or in whole, in any form or by any means, or circulated, without the express written consent of the Publisher and/or the Author. The unauthorized reproduction or distribution of a copyrighted work is illegal. Criminal copyright infringement, including infringement without monetary gain, is investigated by the FBI and is punishable by fines and federal imprisonment.

Last Man Standing
The Legendary Chi-Lites
Featuring Marshall Thompson
by Marshall Thompson

Introduction and Additional Transcriptions
by Dane Ladwig

Edited by Bonnie Classen

Editions available:
Trade Paperback, Hardcover, Kindle (mobi), Nook (epub), and Audiobook

Dedication and Thanks

There are many people in my life I would like to thank for their kind words of encouragement and generous support spanning a lifelong career from the late 1950's to the present. My wife, Tara Thompson, has been my inspiration and my best friend, and for that, I am grateful. As for my fans, I would like to thank each and every one of them for their incredible faith in our music and continued devotion in following the Chi-Lites throughout the years. To the many business associates–turned friends–that I met along the journey and to the many fellow entertainers I had the privilege to share the stage with, I am forever grateful.

The intent of this book is not to merely string a bunch of words into sentences; it is considerably more. Along with our music, it is the legacy I leave behind. I dedicate the pages of this book to each member of the Chi-Lites. Although I am the only surviving original member of the Chi-Lites, and the Last Man Standing, throughout my life, every member has continued to join me on stage and has remained in our music and traveled from my heart to the hearts of our fans through our music. I dedicate this book to the everlasting memory of each member of the Chi-Lites. May the memories we shared and the mark we left upon this world remain a hallmark to the future musicians and entertainers of this world.

—Marshall Thompson

INTRODUCTION BY AUTHOR DANE LADWIG

In 1968, a group of four black teenagers from the Chicago Soul arena auditioned with Carl Davis of Brunswick Records. Carl liked what he heard and he decided to record the quartet. They cut a single (45 LP) titled, "Give It Away." Eugene "Gene" Record and Carl Davis corroborated and co-wrote the song. The quartet's first single quickly rose to a Top 10 hit. Carl knew he had a hit with the band and signed them for a recording deal. "Give It Away," took the quartet to the Apollo Theater in New York City, NY. As they took the stage, they were introduced as the newest sensation to come out of Chicago – The Chi-Lites.

Once innovators in R&B and Pop music, the Chi-Lites and leading legend, Marshall Thompson, set trends in the music industry for generations to come. With their unique vocal arrangements, synchronized choreography, and stylistic stage presence, they inspired the music industry; and musicians around the globe began to take notice of this vocal quartet emerging from of Chicago, Illinois in the early 1960's.

The age of Pop music was given birth when, as fate would have it, Marshall Thompson, Eugene "Gene" Record, Robert "Squirrel" Lester, and Creadel "Red" Jones, crossed one another's paths. It was as if the stars were aligned in harmonic convergence and music was on the cusp of ushering social change in keeping pace with society's demands for Cultural Revolution. In essence, the Chi-Lites fractured the barriers of music segregation.

The Chi-Lites confronted the long-standing apartheid held by social degradation of America's separatism in the music industry. Country music had its devoted Caucasian followers, and Rock & Roll was threatening the moral virtue of the fervent and dedicated patriarchal authoritarian of the domesticated parental figures holding strong to their beliefs and convictions that Rock & Roll was, "A tool of the devil." R&B had deep-seated roots in the African-American communities across the nation. I never forgot reading that Billboard Magazine created the term Rhythm & Blues back in 1948 to replace the words "race music." They also coined the phrase "Soul music." Appropriately, even in the 40's, it was about taking the "race" out of music.

The Chi-Lites followed suit. They discovered a new sound, a new look, and a unique way to traverse the bridge of intolerance and racial tension. By establishing creative and imaginative harmonies, they were anything but unoriginal. Pop music was created and now the audience was uncolored; the boundaries of race had been infiltrated, and what's more, people of all colors loved the music of the Chi-Lites.

When the Chi-Lites released "(For God Sake) Give More Power to the People)" in 1970, and the message was one of a unified people in the face of the ongoing Vietnam War, they joined a very small group of entertainers who were bold enough to speak out publicly against the ongoing travesty in Vietnam. When the song was played on Soul Train, and aired to a national audience, it received acclaimed notoriety. People stood unified to proclaim they wanted "More Power."

It was 1971 and the Chi-Lites would go on to record a song that went to number one, to the surprise of many, with a unique never-before attempted variation; a long monologue as the intro. "Have You Seen Her," was the first of its kind ever to be recorded and pressed and was met with success. Others attempted to open with monologues, even inserting monologues in the middle or the end of songs but they never succeeded in pulling off what came naturally for the Chi-Lites.

Then in the same year, 1971, the songwriter of the Chi-Lites, Eugene Record, wrote a song to his wife about a man lost without his love. "Oh Girl" rose to the top of the charts and became an instant hit. The Chi-Lites were now Pop music stars. They did not sing in segregated tones of black and white; their music was instrumental in breaking down the racial barriers that held America, and the world captive for centuries. The Civil Rights Movement with the Chi-Lites as advocates for their plight recognized their ever-important role in revolutionizing America.

Marshall Thompson, the Last Man Standing, of the original Chi-Lites stands as a monument to political, social, cultural and personal change. He has been revered by many in the entertainment industry as the hardest working person in music and the most admired stage presence in Pop music. Known in his circle as "The Godfather of Pop," Marshall Thompson has "seen it all," and endured every test. His peers have emulated his every move, and sought out his professional business appraisal and guidance.

When the Chi-Lites took the stage people took notice as they sung in unison; sometimes as a single voice; and with difficulty in identifying where one of the vocal masters left off and another came in. That's how tight they were. They captured people's attention with flash and panache, and a touch of class. Wearing their hearts on their sleeves these four gents from Chicago poured their souls out to the world. It's no wonder that they contributed in such monumental fashion; they represented what every adult, child, musician, and business executive aspired for – unrestrained free thinking and resolute moral character with a plan, and a message, that no one and nothing could stop.

I have had the pleasure of meeting Mr. Thompson. I can tell you, from a small boy on the south side of Chicago, to a celebrity, Marshall Thompson has never forgotten his roots and he is one of the most humble and kind persons I have ever met. My life is enriched for knowing Marshall Thompson. He has an exceptional gift, is colorblind to a fault, and his heart knows no bounds. As the last alive and remaining member, and the driving force of the Chi-Lites for decades, Marshall Thompson has shared a wonderful gift with the entertainment and music industry – himself.

The Chi-Lites, with Marshall Thompson as their driving force, will forevermore be remembered for music of inspiration and love expressed through the messages in their songs. The Vocal Group Hall of Fame inducted the Chi-Lites as legends in R&B, Pop, and Soul music, in 2005. They joined other celebrated groups, many of whom they had the distinct pleasure and honor of performing with over their many years in the entertainment industry. Our generation, and generations to come, have benefited from the influence of four black teenagers, who never turned their backs on their dreams, and endured and persevered to unshackle Americans from the chains of intolerance that imprisoned not only the black populations in the US, but the white communities as well.

In closing, if there is one lasting impression that I can glean from my friendship with Mr. Thompson and also growing up listening to the music of the Chi-Lites it is this; long live entertainers, bands, and groups that heed to a higher moral cause allowing their art and discipline to be used to further a greater purpose. That is the stuff legends are made of!

—Dane Ladwig

Contents

Dedication	5
Introduction	7
Through the Looking Glass: The Chi-Lites in Retrospect – by Marshall Thompson	13
Chapters 1-15 Narration	*15*
Genealogy & Roots: The Legendary Chi-Lites and the Chi-Town Sound by Dane Ladwig…	95
The Origin of Pop Music	*97*
The Truth Behind The Rage (The Black Panther Movement)	*101*
The Chi-Lites: Demise of Motown – Corky "The Galoot" – the Mob Connection – Rico – Rise of the "Chi-Sound"	*103*
Tommy's "Boy's"	*109*
The Truth About the Early Years and Beyond	*113*
"Red" Jones and Thompson: Natural Death or ?	*121*
"It's a Wrap": Conclusion	*125*
Inspirational Messages from Friends and Supporters of the Chi-Lites	129
Biographic and Historic Information	143
Appendix	150

Through the Looking Glass:

The Chi-Lites in Retrospect – by Marshall Thompson

> *"We started out singing together back in elementary school and we continued into high school; that's when we became the Desideros. We have great life-long memories together, and I want to express a congratulations to my brother, Marshall. Wishing you many more years of success. Your brother…"*
>
> ~ Del Brown (Tenor singer of the Desideros)

(1)

I still remember the magic of holding drumsticks in my hands for the first time. I had grown accustomed to watching all the great entertainers and privileged that many were either in my family, or members of my family played in their bands. But to actually hold the hickory and feel its smooth slim body and the crown-like tip where the thrills and the enchantment come to life was captivating to a child who was barely out of diapers.

I've always loved the beat. Whenever I would see a band, I always thought, drummers were the coolest, the smoothest cats in the band. That was me, I wanted to be cool and smooth – the man in charge of the beat.

I was born into music. Everyone in my family was immersed in it. It was an unspoken agreement; you had to play an instrument, any instrument. It didn't matter if it was a guitar or a keyboard, as long as you learned and played.

I played the drums at the Regal Theater; it was my induction to the stage. Playing drums backing Gladys Knight & the Pips, and the Staple Singers gave me recognition as a musician. I was influenced heavily by doo-wop sounds and angelic harmonies.

That was the sound we replicated for the Chi-Lites;

conveying a message overflowing with love. Our signature songs like, "Have You Seen Her" and "Oh Girl," truly expressed the heart-felt meaning of our music. But times weren't always good. The realities of life and its hardships were reflected in our music, and the journey continues through this book, sharing the good times and bad, paying tribute to some of the greatest men and women I have had the privilege to call friends; and presenting a side of Marshall Thompson and the Chi-Lites that few people have experienced.

Growing up around musicians and stars, you sort of just fit in with the crowd of talent and become familiar with the stage and entertaining, or you drop out and go your merry way never having evolved. I was not about to walk away, not even as a child. And believe me, sometimes I thought about playing ball, but the only sticks I really wanted in my hands were those sweet, old hickory sticks.

I started out small: a bass drum, a snare drum, one tom-tom, and a cymbal. Nothing like the gigantic sets drummers use today. When I got good enough I graduated to using a high-hat, and it was cool when I played with brushes and we would jam to a smooth jazz tune or a real gutsy blues melody.

Yeah, everyone in the Chi-Lites was musically inclined. We all contributed in big ways to make the right sound; that perfectly balanced melody that was all-inclusive expressing the love we felt in our hearts, and the thoughts we had in our heads. It was a magical sound and a driving force in Pop music. As crisp as the morning dew and as sweet as the most satisfying dessert.

In my days attending school, I was admired by most of the guys, and the girls were crazy about me. I say "most" of the guys because there were some who resented me when their girl would get all honey-eyed on me. While attending DuSable High School in Chicago, there were fun times; most of the girls would straight out flirt with me even if their guy was right beside them. I felt weird about that, but a lot of times the guy would just stand there and be all friendly with me and want to hang out. I was real popular. It was like if they could hang out with me, their girlfriend would like them more or something.

The girls threw themselves at me. And honestly, at times, I was grateful for it, because I have always been a lover, not a fighter. At other times I was uncomfortable, especially if I already had a girl I was interested in, or someone I was seeing. All that attention could be overwhelming.

Getting into fights never concerned me. For some reason all the gangs showed up at our concerts and they loved our music. It was no secret that every gang in Chicago embraced the Chi-Lites and each member of the band individually. We never connected with a single gang, but if you messed with the Chi-Lites, you would first have to go through the gangs – and nobody was crazy or stupid enough to do that.

With my Christian upbringing I never even considered getting into fights or becoming involved with the gangs, but for some guys, that's the only life they knew. They respected my decision and I respected theirs. I was sad because I knew where their lives were headed, but I never once treated them any differently for the choices they made.

Mama was the religious one in the family. She made sure straight away that we learned right from wrong – and knew that God's love for us would carry us through the darkest of times. She was the strongest person I ever knew – a driven woman with the force of God's love behind her. I am a lot like momma was!

"The songs the Chi-Lites recorded stood the test of time. With Marshall Thompson's leadership, the Chi-Lites will never die. My hat's off to you Marshall."

~ Gene Chandler (The Duke of Earl)

(2)

I never measured success the way other people did. To me, I became a success when I was able to do my mom and my dad proud. I remember the day I was able to provide mom with some nice things; nice clothes, a car, and a house. I finally started to support her and gave back for all that she sacrificed over the years to keep me going. She was a single mom, raising three kids, and the time had come that I made sure she didn't want for anything.

As far as my papa, I recall the proudest day of our lives; it was when I went to visit him during a gig he had in Calumet City. Back in those days it was considered a top-notch club. I was now "of age;" at eighteen I was able to get into the clubs.

When the door opened, dad was playin' the piano watching me out of the corner of his eye. Mid-song, he stopped playin' and switched songs. I immediately recognized the tune; it was, "Have You Seen Her." Dad put his own spin on it.

Do doot doot, do do doot, doot doot... Do doot doot, do do doot, doot doot... Here comes my son... Have You Seen *Him?*

I got all choked up. That knocked me out. "Have You Seen Her," was at the top of the charts; and I was dressed sharp, I had money, I knew I had made it to the big times; but when my pops introduced me, and everyone in the place went wild, I felt good for my dad, 'cause that was my dad, and I knew I had finally attained success in a way that could and would make a difference.

In the 1950's, when music was at a pivotal point in history, we were experimenting with new sounds. It wasn't that we didn't enjoy the music on the scene back then, but we wanted to stand out – we wanted something unlike anything anyone ever heard before. We knew we had talent in the group, and our goal was to get the most out of the gifts we had been given.

The R&B and soul sounds were really great at the time, but deep down we knew that if we were going to stand out we had to discover a whole new sound – an all-encompassing sound that could penetrate the barriers of genre and of color, and we knew that accomplishing that was going to be a near-impossible mission.

Breaking down the walls, and overcoming the obstacles, was our biggest fear at the time. The stage had been set; now it was time to step up to the microphone. Creadel "Red" Jones and myself played with the group, The Desideros. Eugene Record, Robert "Squirrel" Lester who was nicknamed "Squirrel" as a child because of his agility and ability to climb trees, and Clarence Johnson from the Chanteurs teamed up with us in the early 60's and we were going by the name the "Hi-Lights." We wanted our group name to stand out and reflect a certain devotion and love for Chicago, so in '64 we changed the name to "Marshall and the Chi-Lites." But later that year Clarence decided to move on, and we decided to shorten the name to the "Chi-Lites."

It was like we wanted people to focus on the music and not just on one band member, so I was genuinely okay with not having my name preceding the band's name. It was a collaborative effort and everybody in the band deserved to be recognized for their contribution. We were more like a family than a business anyway, and we loved and respected one another. It was all about unity.

After we shortened the name to the Chi-Lites, people were lovin' it; and we realized that for us to stand out from all the rest we were going to have to get into some choreography, synchronized dancing, and dressing alike on stage. We wanted people to notice and remember us. Once that was figured out, we moved on to deciding how the music could stand out more... become even more memorable.

It was all about style. You either had it or you didn't. I remember when I would play drums for Gladys Knight; the Pips had style, they all dressed alike, and on stage they moved as a unit – kind of like an army platoon in boot camp walking in unison. And that's what we wanted for the Chi-Lites.

"Marshall Thompson and the Chi-Lites accomplished a great deal over the years. And Marshall did so much for me and my family. He is the type of person who will do anything for anybody, and help – no questions asked. Marshall is a loveable guy and he is truly the Last great Man Standing. Marshall helped my family in a time of great need. He was there as he always was.
   Best of Luck"
      ~ Joe Jackson (Father of the famous Jackson family)

(3)

A day doesn't go by when I don't think about Red (Creadel "Red" Jones), Squirrel (Robert "Squirrel" Lester) and Gene (Eugene "Gene" Record) and all the guys that followed and became a part of the Chi-Lites. Thinking about my friends triggers thoughts about when we got together and first started playin' as the Chi-Lites.

We were just a bunch of overconfident kids with ambitions and pie-in-the-sky dreams of making it someday. Although I always knew we would hit it big, you're never really prepared until it happens. Most folks would consider cuttin' a record and hearing their music on the radio as "the big time," but for me, for us, it was different.

We were surrounded by music all our lives and, for the most part, our families were always kickin' it with celebrities. To be in the spotlight was not something special or out of the ordinary for us, but that's not to say it's not an exceptional or distinctive honor to become a celebrity. It's just that we viewed celebrities the same way we viewed most everything else – it's just what you did because it was what was expected of you, to become someone and play your music to your full potential.

When we considered what we wanted to present in the music, we were faced with some major obstacles. People were used to R&B and Soul, but when it came to Pop music we were going to attempt something never before tried. Black folks were not accustomed to hearing classical instrumentation in our music. We were breaking new territory with our music, and didn't really know if it would catch on, but we wanted to have a distinctive sound… a sound like no other.

We were all seasoned musicians and that helped us to expand the music. To mix the R&B, the Soul, and bring something new to the table was quite a challenge. The words would make a connection to the heart. The choreography would help to make a connection to the fans. But the music and harmony had to engage the heart, the soul, and the very being of the person listening to the song.

There are songs where we have only four instruments playing in the background, and there are others where we had an entire orchestra accompanying us. It was wild. I've heard people say time and time again that our music is "heaven sent," and I humbly agree. There's some kind of divine inspiration in our songs. I can feel it.

I've been told that I am "the hardest working man in show business," but I don't think of it that way. How can I consider doing what I love as "hard" work? It's my passion in life and I feel honored to have been given the privilege to do what I love.

The members of the Chi-Lites have always been like a family to me. Whenever they were down and out, so was I. That's when I would cut jokes and do whatever I could to pick them up. And when they were up I was right there along with them. We were inseparable in my eyes and in my heart. So if they needed anything, anything at all, I was there for them, and they were there for me. That's just how it went. You could say we were the Chi-Lites gang, but without the violence of a gang. There was camaraderie and loyalty. That pretty much sums it up.

That same mentality of brotherhood and family extended to each of our families and friends. They saw us as sons, brothers, and so on. They didn't treat us like business partners or copartners; we were just "the boys," and when we gained notoriety and we became well-known they were proud to introduce us as the Chi-Lites, and we, in turn were delighted that they were so proud.

The reception we received following a television appearance was out of this world. People lined up for blocks just to welcome us home. Back at my high school they made a big deal out of me attending there, and to this day, whenever I visit, I get the warmest welcome you could imagine.

"The year was 1960, the place – Chicago. A group came from the Windy City known as the Chi-Lites. With Marshall Thompson as the group's leader, singer, and spokesperson, they racked up 11 top 10 singles. At this time, Marshall stands as the lone survivor of the legendary Chi-Lites, but the memories live on through him."

~ Jay Johnson, Morning DJ – The Touch Radio Network.

(4)

Many people are aware that I am writing this book while I am in the hospital following a massive stroke, and I will elaborate more on that later. Despite life's challenges, and the obstacles thrown in my path, I will never stop. That's just the type of guy I am. As I've said before, I am driven. I can't fully explain the drive, but I have fully embraced it over the years.

People have mistaken my drive for lust of the spotlight or greed, but nothing could be further from the truth. I think offering anything short of my very best would simply be giving up on myself and the things I so passionately believe in.

That's why over the span of my career, I did all I could to keep the Chi-Lites in the public eye, including replacing band members who left or had passed on. It was, and still is, important to me to keep their memory alive, keep our songs playin' on the radio, and continue touring.

Here I am at the hospital and it's time for my therapy session. I've always been a survivor and this, too, I will survive. However, I know now that I'll soon be singing with the original Chi-Lites again, and that doesn't scare me. I look forward to singing in God's choir. I don't think He'll allow me to work so many hours though.

The hardest time in recent years was when I had to bury a very close friend, who was more a family member than a friend. I still struggle to accept that he has gone on to be with his maker.

On June 25, 2009, when I got the call from Joe (Jackson) that Michael (Jackson) was found dead, I was devastated. I thought, my God, not Michael. I watched him grow up. He was like a son to me. I immediately joined the family at Michael's place in Los Angeles. It was unreal. I kept thinking, there's got to be some kind of mistake. I was waiting for Michael to come out of his room, like so many times before, smile and say, "Hi Uncle Marshall." But all I was greeted with was medics and police, and my heart shattered.

Even at the funeral when I was sitting in the front with the entire Jackson family (they consider me family and they always have), I still didn't feel like Michael had been taken from us. I kept thinking that I would turn around and find Michael sitting behind us.

Well, I am not going to debate the investigation; that's not what this book is about, but I will say that there is much that was twisted and many untruths that were manufactured to promote the media. We, the family, know the truth. Michael was disgraced publicly and that tragic story could fill another book. The fact is, Michael is at rest now, and his family, and I, miss him very much. Too many of my friends have passed on.

I have been privileged to have been embraced and supported by some of the most incredible people in the business. Back in '71 the Chi-Lites appeared on Soul Train, and American Bandstand. Both Don (Cornelius) and Dick (Clark) said we would hit it big on the charts and indeed we did. I became very close friends with both of these icons of the music industry; even then, we knew that if either one of them liked our music, we would make it big. As it turned out, both Dick and Don loved the Chi-Lites' music.

Over the years, we made repeat appearances on Soul Train, and American Bandstand. In the '70's that was about as "big" and famous as you could get. We went from opening shows for Gladys Knight and the Pips, Roberta Flack, James Brown, Stevie Wonder and so many others, to being headliners with bands opening for our shows. Becoming the headliner was the sign of accomplishment every group craves. That's when you know you've made it to the "Big's."

"(Don) Cornelius took a show (Soul Train) featuring the Chi-Lites to California, which led to the national syndication."
ABC 7 Eyewitness News Feb 2, 2012

(5)

*B*ack in the early 70's Don (Cornelius) and I were tight. He asked if he could feature us on his show, move it out of Chicago to California, and to a national platform. We were excited about it and we really hoped Don's expectations would be met. But deep down, we wondered if the world, outside of Chicago, was ready for four black dudes from the hood changing music so radically. But radical is exactly what was needed at that time.

The 60's was a time of tension and struggle for everyone. The black community carried with it the chains of oppression and inequality. The white people just wanted the war in Vietnam to come to an end and for their young boys, husbands and fathers to come home. What we would do would mark a defining moment not only with our music, but in history as well.

It was important to hook up with people in the business like Don, and Herb Kent (Producer), who understood the dynamics involved in a changing climate, and how our music would affect race relations. It was not just important, it was essential.

Don "got it" and that's why he featured both black and white bands with an audience of mixed races. We were not just making a statement or revolting, we were retraining the way people were raised to think; and giving both black and white people messages of hope, inspiration and love.

At times, the ignorance and resistance was nearly unbearable. But the things we endured were surely for a higher cause, a global cause; and the segregation had to die. Our music was the best avenue to reach masses of people to send a message, and in time they responded. Slowly but steadily the hostility and conflicts subsided, and our cause prevailed. People tried to say we were militant, just because we played at Black Panther parties and they took our song *(For God Sake) Give More Power to the People*, and made it into their slogan. They watched our backs, gave us protection, people knew not to fool with the Chi-Lites or they would have some very serious problems. I mean, we knew them, and hung out with them, but that's all. In retrospect, even if we were involved, it was worth every bit of the effort and trouble just to be unified, and in harmony with our white brothers and sisters.

See, I might have roots in R&B and Soul, but Pop music – back then – was colorblind. "For God's Sake, Give More Power to the People (1971)," really broke things open for us with record sales (our first million seller album), and people of all races were hangin' on to the hope and the message of the song. It gave them something to think about, things to consider about real life.

We were still uncertain that the world was "primed" for our message of love and peace in a time of destruction and uneasiness. Don stood behind us and we were successful despite the world's issues. I think in many ways we were embraced as a direct result of the matters going on around us. Either way, it worked out, and here I am six decades later still telling the story and Rockin' and Rollin'!

"I am very proud to be a member of this organization for almost 30 years. We have toured around the world singing, entertaining and meeting our many wonderful fans. The reality that I am singing with the Chi-Lites, a group that I have loved since the first time I heard them has been a dream come true. I would never have believed that I would be living a 'dream come true.' Thank you, Marshall, for embracing me and allowing me to be a part of the Chi-Lites. You have surpassed all plans and expectations that Squirrel, Gene, Red and yourself, laid out over 50 years ago. God's blessing to you, my good friend."

Frank "Tachallah" Reed (8-16-1954 – 2-26-2014)
Lead vocalist of the Chi-Lites 1988 – 2014
(Successor to former lead singer Eugene "Gene" Record)

(6)

Frank and I go way back. The funny thing is, when Gene was leaving the group I was introduced to Frank and the person who introduced him said, "He sounds just like Gene. You can't tell them apart." I laughed. There was no way I wouldn't be able to tell if it was Gene or a stand in; I spent too many years singin' with Gene not to be able to know the difference.

Frank comes walking in. He's all decked out and sportin' a big hat. I'm all about hats; they just make you look right when you got your stage outfits on. I wear mine all the time. Even when I go to the store or to the restaurant, you'll never catch me without a hat – it's my thing.

So here's this guy and he's standing there all kind of suave and sophisticated. He has this coolness about him. The look in his eyes says, I'm serious, I can handle anything, and I am "Mr. Cool." He picks up the microphone, hangs his head down, and as soon as the music starts, he demands everyone's immediate attention. Mr. Cool just turned into Mr. Hot. His moves on stage were identical to ours. As soon as he opened his mouth and the tone hit the microphone, I sat down in the nearest chair and was spellbound.

If I squinted or turned my head, I would have thought Gene was at the mic. I was sitting there in awe. This cat they called "Tachallah" was a dead ringer for Gene. After Frank finished the song, he walked toward me. "Hey kid," I said, "you're really good." "Tachallah" smiled. I shook his hand, leaned in, and said, "Looks like we got us a new lead singer."

Frank fit right in and the guys loved him, he sounded so much like Gene. Even when I mistakenly called him Gene a few times he would look over at me and smile or give me a wink just to let me know we was cool. He was an easy going kind of guy like that.

I am like that too. It takes an awful lot to ruffle my feathers. I figure, what's the sense in getting angry about something. It's not going to change anything. Getting upset won't take back what was done so I figure let's skip the mad part, deal with the issue, and fix the problem. If I got rattled about all the stuff that happened when we were trying to make a name for ourselves, it would have kept us from moving forward, and we might have never advanced from practicing in the garage or basement.

When I was on the Soul Train Cruise and I got the message that Frank had passed away from a heart attack, I couldn't tell anybody. That's the way I am, and that's the way Frank was. The show must go on. If I would have allowed myself to feel the pain in my heart before the show then I would have probably met up with Frank at heaven's gates. Instead I kept it inside and waited until after the show.

My heart was broken when Frank passed away, but I am grateful that he and I had the privilege to know and love one another. Perhaps keeping things bottled up inside led to my stroke, but in a sense it was a blessing in disguise. This "interruption" and challenge gave me time to reflect on my life including: my spiritual life, my business attitude, and the friends and loved ones that have enriched my life. It also gave me the "down time" necessary to work on this book.

That's another quality Frank and I shared; there's no dwelling on the negative. I had a stroke. I don't look for pity or misplaced empathy. I look for ways I can use what happened to better my life and the lives of the people I come in contact with. To me, that's called making a positive difference, and that attitude should carry over into every facet of a person's life.

"You have put in a lot of hard work into the music business. I commend you for sticking with it, not everybody has the ability to succeed the way you have. Keep on pushing, brother! God bless. Your brother for life…"
> Ron Tyson, Tenor vocalist of the Temptations
> (1983–current) replacing the late Eddie Kendricks

(7)

There were so many things going on back in the beginning with the Chi-Lites. I really don't think any of us could sense exactly what the impact was going to be. We knew the music was going to hit it big, but you know, as far as four black dudes breaking into the white market, that was all new territory.

I remember in the 70's when America was glued to the television and everyone, black and white, was going crazy over the mini-series Roots (ABC – written by Alex Haley). Now that was good TV, and I was thrilled about the nine Emmy Awards it won. But folks were saying things like, for the first time in the history of the African-American people the [black] actors and actresses finally made a mark in entertainment.

At that time, I was happy for the success of the show, but I couldn't help but think that this was not the first time African-Americans made their mark. The Chi-Lites had been makin' their mark since the late 1950's. I pondered that thought for a while.

Could it be… the Chi-Lites, and other groups, actors and entertainers, who may not have received the critical acclaim that the cast of Roots received, have been pioneers in paving the path for the acceptance of such a powerful movie? The way I saw it, we were kind of like the first gold miners setting the stage for the gold rush.

When I thought of it in those terms, I felt pretty darn good for mine, and our, contributions to altering, enhancing, and being instrumental in the evolvement of the music entertainment industry almost four decades ago.

There were many people sayin' that we were successful because we were connected to organized crime. Granted, our last days with Brunswick were shadowed as a consequence of their connections to certain thugs and criminals, but we were never caught up in that racket. Tommy (reputed mobster Gaetano Vastola), ran things and he helped us out, [he] got us exposure, so when he said to do this show or to do that one, we just did it, no questions asked.

The problem came when The Big Guy (a nickname used by Gaetano Vastola), was busted by the fed's, and then Brunswick Records was taken down too. That's when we got dragged into the middle of things, but we were cool. There was nothing they could pin on us, they wanted to drag us in, but they knew we was clean.

You know when Nat (Tarnapol) was managing Jackie (Wilson), after he left Decca and came to Brunswick, Morris (Levy, known as the "God Father of Music," as he ran the industry), was really pissed. Then when Jackie left Brunswick, Carl (Davis, owner and producer of Brunswick Records), and came to Chi-Town to record on our label, Carl and Morris, were really pissed. They knew it wasn't Nat behind the changes, Nat was taking his orders from Tommy – The Big Guy.

Everyone thought Carl was pissed at us, but it was not us, it was directions that we got from much higher places, and we had to follow the orders, no questions asked. That's just the way it was. Our hands were tied, and if we wanted to continue to be contenders in the music business, we knew the score.

"I was so deeply in love with her that I didn't know if I could continue to go on living with the same drive and compassion I knew without my Connie at my side."
  Marshall Thompson (On losing his wife Constance "Connie" Thompson)

(8)

My darkest days were back in 1997. We had just finished playing a concert in Pennsylvania. The show was a hit. We were all tired and we were driving back home to Chicago. Our driver, Ray (Raymond Foreman) was always spot on; we never had reason to worry about him or his reliability in getting us to the shows on time. Then suddenly it felt like we were in one of those big dryers at the laundromat flying and tumbling about in the car. I was scared 'cause I dozed off and didn't know what happened. When the car finally stopped rolling, I realized we just flipped over.

  I looked around and everybody was moaning. I could tell that Frank (Reed) was hurt; he was in a lot of pain. Squirrel (Robert Lester) got a little banged up, but he was okay, and Ray seemed to be okay. I didn't seem to be hurt from what I could tell at that time. I looked over to check on Connie and I knew right away it was not good; Connie was not in the car.

  I'll never forget that stretch of interstate 80; it still haunts my dreams. I didn't get any physical injuries but inside, I was seriously wounded. My heart and soul were fractured and my very being was in shock.

  I can tell you the only thing running through my mind at the time is Connie is my universe. She looked out for us while we were on the road and she was our manager. She sang and harmonized on backup vocals, and was the glue that held us together. I met her when I was already famous, but that didn't seem to faze her. She didn't judge a person by what they had, she cared more about who a person was; what made them tick, what their passions were, and what their character was like.

In many ways, Connie groomed me for the audience. She advised me when something was going to work and when it wasn't, when to get rid of a certain step or to rethink an outfit. She was really tuned into the music scene. Although I consider myself very smart when it comes to the entertainment business, compared to Connie I was a pupil, a student she taught how to learn the ropes of life and also the business we were in.

We were so "connected" that I would begin a thought in my head, and before I could fully process it, Connie would blurt out the solution or finish what I had already been thinking. It was much more than intuition; it was as if our souls and brains were fused together. She could just know a thing about me, and me about her, without ever speaking a single word, or discussing our feelings, and we could communicate automatically without being present in the same room – or the same city.

I suppose that's what true love really is. We started our relationship with no expectations; neither of us begrudged one another our faults, and we embraced one another's shortcomings. Most of all, without question, we knew we could depend and rely on each other always. Connie and I were married for 27 years. We were so close, and I was so deeply in love with her that I didn't know if I could continue on with the same drive, ambition and compassion without my Connie at my side. In fact, I wasn't even sure I could continue on.

To see her lying on the ground where she was ejected

from the car was the most terrifying sight I had ever endured. I am grateful for my time with Connie; I know that she still watches over me. In my own way, I have carried her legacy with me as I have conducted business over the years. She was the finest example of a leader in the music business I have ever known and I have tried to follow her example.

On that horrible day in 1997, when I lost Connie, I wrote the song "Hold On To Your Dreams" in her honor. I praise God that I had my time with Connie, and that he spared the rest of us for His plan although that's the thing about trusting in God's plan, I didn't understand why it happened. I still don't. But that's why it's called faith. I trust that God had a reason, otherwise Connie's death and Frank's surgery having a metal plate surgically inserted in his back, and my emotional scars would be all a result of nothingness, and that just doesn't make any sense.

"Soul music. I'd [like to] bring back soul music and it would be the only music you'd hear on the radio. Just so much music from that era that I absolutely love. My God, the O'Jays, the Dramatics, the Chi-Lites. I listen to a lot of that kind of radio. It's my favorite."

Seamus Deaver – Interview April 2014 (ABC's Castle Lounge) Actor ~ Castle, CSI, General Hospital, Hollywoodland, Monkey Love, NCIS, Outside the Law, Ready or Not, That 70's Show, and many more.

(9)

A few weeks back, I overheard these two fella's saying it was easier to break into the music scene during the music "explosion" of the 50's and 60's then it is today. I wanted to set them straight, but the gentleman I am, I reserved my comments as I was not invited to their philosophic debate about the music business. I will say here, however, that their assumptions couldn't have been any further from the truth.

They argued that back then the music business was primed for any musician to simply walk off the street and cut a record, and that if they had even the slightest talent or a unique sound that set them apart, they could "easily" make a hit record. I can say from personal experience that it takes a lot more effort.

To make the charts back then wasn't just about being different, but also having a forceful drive both on stage and in a business sense. It was not just about cutting a record, hopping on a tour bus, playing venues, and partying till the early morning hours after a show. That's the Hollywood movie version.

The real version, if you want to become a success and

remain on the charts, takes dedication and devotion. It's about making perfect music, and much more. The business side is about drive. The drive is the difference that will set one group above, or below, another group. The reason that my good friends, the Rolling Stones, and entertainers like my dear friend, Roberta Flack, continue to fill venues to standing-room-only capacity, is their drive.

Drive consist of many things like ambition, determination, effort, energy, force, hustle, initiative, and motivation. Become complacent or idle, and you will certainly decline on the charts; and if you are not on the charts, people won't remember who you are. That, my friends, is the name of the music game; making sure people remember you and your music. I cut my first record over fifty years ago and people still remember who I am, who the Chi-Lites are, and they know many of our songs – word for word.

Part of what you must be driven to accomplish is gaining what I refer to as the "power." The power is what drives you to promote your music and the only sure fire way of gaining that power; is by making connections. Not just any connections but connections that count. Joe, down at the drug store, might buy your records once you've released them, however, Joe will not get you an introduction to the big record producer that owns a major record label five states away.

Network, make connections, and make them often. Don't assume that you will be "discovered." You need to do some footwork for that to happen. Contact your local radio station and get on the good side of the DJ. Enter worthwhile talent contests that give you some recognition. If you know of a local talent that has hit it big, find out where they hang out, bring a karaoke machine and sing. Do anything, but be heard!

The other thing you need when considering if you are going to make it in music is talent. Everybody thinks they have what it takes when they sing in the shower, but it's a very different world out there when you are on stage or in the studio. To determine if you have genuine talent, the best gauge is in the ear of the beholder. What are the professionals and general audience saying about your talent?

From time to time, I have watched the talent search shows on prime time television. Some of the talent that is discovered blows my mind. Like any profession, any specialized field, professional training is required. Some people are born with "gifts" and even those need skilled tweaking and polishing. Skip the training and you may as well stay in the shower.

Okay, so you have the drive, and you have the talent. Now what do you do to get the deal? In this day and age; it is an absolute necessity to learn about marketing. The internet is every artist's or musician's best friend. Social networks and the marketing tools they offer provide a powerful platform to make a difference in self promotion.

Musician Alex Day from Sussex, England, made a half-million dollars last year simply by selling his independently released songs on the internet. Rapper Mac Miller (Malcom James McCormick), sold 150 albums in one week on the internet. Both of these musicians met with success because they were thinking "outside the box," and they used creative marketing skills to promote their music.

Getting back to the original argument by the two fellas. Was it easier to break into the music scene in the 50's-60's or today? I believe it is much easier to break into music today than it ever was before. It merely takes drive, talent, and marketing skills. If you have those three things, you may step out of the shower and onto the stage.

"I am a former gang member who turned my life around because Marshall Thompson exposed me to another side of life. Through his encouragement and support, I am currently working with violent gang members and the poverty stricken on Chicago's streets to provide new beginnings. Marshall unselfishly and single-handedly took his message and music to the impoverished, offering them hope. He offered inner-city youth access to his personal resources: producers, rehearsal space, studio, studio-engineers, and radio and media outlets. Marshall Thompson's dedication and support for our cause to fight poverty and violence in the African-American community has reflected his love for his people and society."

Floyd Davis
Co-founder of Woodlawn Battle on Wax for Peace, Inc.

(10)

Just doin' my time! And that was exactly what I wanted to do. It was 2001, and I was working as a police officer in the Park District. I always admired the police, and making it to the level of an officer was a dream come true. To serve and protect was, to me, one of the most admirable qualities a person could aspire to.

To make a long story short, I was in the wrong place at the wrong time. I don't blame anyone but myself, and I deserved the penalty I paid. The time in my life that I consider a very prestigious time also turned out to be one of the darkest and most humbling experiences of my life. It was an experience I wished many times I could have the opportunity to do over, and stay clear of certain people and situations.

A lot of musicians who ended up in jail later wrote about it in their songs. My music was not about jail and stuff like that. I didn't need any new experiences to write or sing about, and I definitely was not going to entertain the idea of writing songs about the experience.

I should have been less trusting. I have never lied, and this was no exception. When I took the stand I told the prosecution exactly what my role was; I would pick up envelopes and deliver them to my boss, the Chief of Police, and that was that. They did not believe that I had no idea that the chief was selling badges to people so they could carry guns. So there I was the "bagman" transferring money from point A to the chief who would put it in his "re-election fund."

When the Judge read the court's ruling, "Guilty on all counts of illegally transferring bribery funds," I humbly and respectfully accepted responsibility for my actions and thanked the judge for the verdict. I have always accepted responsibility for my actions, and just because this was a serious situation, I was not going to change who I was.

The institution I was reprimanded to be held at Oxford Federal Correction Institution, is located about 60 miles north of Madison, Wisconsin. I had heard of Oxford, and my attorney said, "… as far as prisons go, Oxford is the vacation spot of all prisons," like that was supposed to offer me reassurance of some sort. At that time, the only recollections I had of prisons were what I saw on television, and what I experienced the few times I visited friends who made the wrong choices and were incarcerated.

The courts allowed me, on my pledge, to drive to the prison. I kept thinking… *This is not going to be a good thing.* When you are going to spend the next year and a day in prison your mind thinks all kinds of strange things.

As it turns out, Oxford is a minimum to medium security facility; it's where all the politicians go when they are sentenced. To be honest, once I walked through the doors and was going through the processing stage, I realized how lucky I was to have ended up here.

At Oxford the cells are more like hotel suites, complete with your very own cable television and all the amenities you would expect at home – remember we are not dealing with rapist and murderers at Oxford, just people who made wrong choices, mostly financially rooted. That's not to say that they are not held to the law, but there is no threat of violence or retribution.

While I was incarcerated, I was permitted a set of drums. The guys on my block really enjoyed listening to me play. I was also actively involved with the religious services offered. I really enjoyed leading men to God in hopes that they would find solace in His word.

There's no denying it, I got what I deserved. I should have been more aware that I was allowing myself to be used – more mindful of the situation I placed myself in. But I am not one to dwell on the past, nor am I one to displace the blame. I was at fault, and the courts acted within the law to enforce it as it pertained to me and my actions. If there is one lesson I learned through the whole mess is, it was to never place myself in a situation without recognizing the consequences to every action and choice I make. Those dark days back in 2001-02, were unnecessary and avoidable.

"If it were not for Marshall, I would have passed by the Jackson 5. It was Marshall who told me, "Put everything on hold and watch these kids." Marshall was responsible for my interest in the Jackson 5 and for them being discovered. I am grateful for Marshall's determination and demanding that I drop what I was doing to discover one of the greatest acts to ever come out of Motown. Thank you, my brother. Peace and love."

Robert "Bobby" Taylor, Little Daddy and the Bachelors, Bobby Taylor and the Vancouver's, Recording Artist, Recording Producer

(11)

There was a time when the Chi-Lites, and I, were real greenhorns in the music business and to the world. We thought the record company paid the taxes on our royalties so we didn't pay the taxes. We learned the hard way that the taxes were our responsibility. We all laughed about this misunderstanding and we had to pay back with penalties too. It was really played up in the media that we were trying to scam the government when we actually didn't know the taxes went unpaid. It was what you could call was an honest mistake. Hey, we had the money, and we paid it back. It really wasn't about the money anyway. It was about four guys making hit records and assuming the record company was taking care of everything.

Despite the rumors that I was involved with bank fraud and record company swindles, that was nothin' but lies. There were even stories that the FBI was investigating me for murder, and it was all just bad PR and attempts to con me into paying money to stop the rumors.

Honestly, I feel sorry for people who attempt to strong-arm celebrities into paying off threats. People like that are really hurting deep down and they need help. I don't mind helping folks; it's what I love to do. I'll give someone my last dime if I see a need, and I am convinced that God wants me to give all I have for the cause. But when someone has a sense of feeling they are owed "just because;" that's not what I consider a legitimate need.

When I was a little boy about 5 or 6 years-old, I worked. I went down to the corner of 47th and St. Lawrence in Chicago, and danced. That's how I worked out my moves and I enjoyed every minute of it. People passin' by would drop nickels and dimes at my feet so I went to the corner every day. That was my first job when I was just a boy. Nobody owed me; I worked for my nickels and dimes, and I loved it.

Not everyone can sing or dance, but everyone has got somethin' in them; some skill or talent that they can use to earn a few bucks. This culture has become a "gimme" civilization and many feel everything is owed to them. They don't realize how amazing and rewarding life can be if they put a little effort into something. It's always, "gimme" this and "gimme" that, and when it's not handed over, they go to extremes and take what they want in a disrespectful manner. Then they dare to act all proud as though they had earned it themselves.

When we were kids, we knew the difference between taking and earning, and the difference between respecting and getting a butt whooping. There's a quote straight out of the Bible, paraphrased it goes like this… "Spare the rod, spoil the child (Proverbs 13:24." And we were not spoiled children in my family!

Soon after Michael (Jackson) passed away, many reports came out of the media. The propaganda and tabloid stories painted Joe (Michael's father) as some kind of unloving monster that assaulted Michael every time he was around. It's odd that these stories come out after someone has passed when they don't have the chance to defend themselves or their loved ones.

The truth is my family and I have known the Jackson's for most of our lives. It was I who got Michael and the Jackson 5 started in the business. This scrawny little kid, Michael, was singin' at schools and Sunday gatherings. A mutual friend who was not in the music business said, "Hey Marshall, you need to hear these kids from Gary (Indiana); they'll blow you away. I thought, ain't no kids gonna blow me away; they need to stick with school talent contests.

My friend brought them to a rehearsal and reluctantly I agreed to listen. When they began to harmonize, I *was* blown away. I immediately sensed that they would be the next big rage and that if they were going to make it in the music business, they needed direction. I partnered them up with Bobby (Taylor). I knew he could shake things up and help them become the big stars they were destined to be. Their music deserved to be shared with the world, and I didn't want to see them be taken advantage of by getting in with the wrong people. The Jacksons, and Michael Jackson, went on to become Pop music icons. The rest is history.

When Michael passed away, and much of the world was still grieving, all manner of tabloid dirt and slander seemed to be dragging his name (and the Jackson name) through the mud. The media turned their attention on Michael's father, Joe. The Jackson kids can tell you, as I can, that Joe loved Michael and still does to this day. Michael was not the victim of anything. The Jackson family can confirm, as they already have, that Joe and

Michael had a normal father and son relationship.

Did Michael get a whooping when he deserved it? Sure he did. However, I have known Joe Jackson nearly all my life, and I have never known him to raise a hand to any of his children in an abusive manner. But I have known the grieving father who has been in turmoil over his son's untimely death, and the unjust treatment he and his family received at the time. I sat with him at Michael's funeral, and listened to him sob, and no matter how you cut it, no parent should have to experience his or her child's death.

"Music has healing power. It has the ability to take people out of themselves for a few hours."

Elton John

(12)

2014 was the coldest and snowiest winter on record in Chicago. It was not a difficult decision to agree to an appearance on the Soul Train Caribbean Cruise trading the dreary Chicago weather for the sunshine and beauty of the tropics in the exotic South Seas.

Many friends would join us and I always loved performing with this particular bunch. I looked forward to visiting with Charlie Wilson, Roberta (Flack), the Isley Brothers, The Commodores, Stephanie (Mills), Peabo (Bryson), Peaches & Herb, and many more friends. With the lineup that was scheduled, I was certain that the cruise and the show would be the most memorable in a long while.

We left the port out of Florida for the 7-day cruise and the overall feelings were of excitement and we were looking forward to a great time. Performances would no doubt be fascinating, but the best part would be enjoying each other's company and having fun doing what we do best – entertaining. A weeklong party, reminiscing, and catching up with all our friends. What could be better than that?

As I expected, the concerts were magnificent and the fans were tremendous. On the last day of the cruise just before heading home, I heard the news about Frank (Reed). I had just talked to him the day before and here I was reading a text that he passed away from a fatal heart attack.

I knew Frank since the 1980's when he joined the Chi-Lites as the lead singer. He did a great job filling in for me and stepping up to the plate to keep things going with the Chi-Lites, when I was in prison. Frank had it rough. In '97 he had to have a permanent metal plate surgically inserted in his back after being ejected from the car when it crashed on the way back from the concert in Pennsylvania, during the same horrific accident that my Constance died.

Frank and I were the only Chi-Lites still standing after a long list of great men had gone on to meet their maker and be with their loved ones. To learn the news of Frank's death was devastating. But... there was one more show to fulfill my obligation to the Soul Train Cruise and the many good folks who traveled far and paid good money to be entertained.

That final show was fantastic. I felt as though I owned the stage. All I kept thinking was... *This has got to be a great show for the people and for Frank; I know he'll be up there on that stage with me.*

I am the type of person who usually holds everything in. I don't like to bother folks with my concerns, and I like to mull things over before I talk about stuff. That night was no different. I didn't even tell my wife Tara that I got a message that Frank had passed away. I felt I had to repress my personal feelings because no matter what the cost, I had always lived by a "show must go on" agenda and I wasn't going to change. I always met my obligations.

After the show I headed back to my stateroom and Tara could sense that something wasn't right. I finally told her about Frank. She asked how I was doing, and I confessed, I wasn't feeling well physically. She called the medic up from the infirmary. They said I appeared to be suffering from dehydration, but should be fine. It seemed ironic; I was, surrounded by billions of gallons of water, yet my body was suffering from a lack of water. It seemed somewhat poetic, but, to me, it still didn't make sense.

A few days went by and I kept feeling worse. Desperate for answers and relief, I was airlifted to a hospital. It didn't take the doctors long to realize that I was not dehydrated, but in fact, I had suffered a massive stroke. I was devastated.

As soon as I was stable, I was transported to a hospital near my home in Chicago, IL. I lost the use of my left side; my arm and leg were paralyzed. My speech was affected, and I knew it was going to be a long road back from this traumatic event. However, I was not about to let this hold me back. I held on to thoughts of my music and how it could help me through this; how it could heal me. Music is my whole life and I was not going to let this stop me from entertaining or singing.

At the hospital, they put me in the children's ward. They do that for celebrities to keep them on a low profile. The doctors didn't want the media swarming around in search of an interview; they wanted me to concentrate on getting well. It was actually a blessing being in the children's ward. I met some fabulous kids in the hospital for those seven weeks. It also reminded me that there is so much more that you and I, can do for the children of this world who are holding onto nothing more than their dreams.

While in physical therapy, I began to regain feeling in my leg. I worked with speech therapists and a song/music therapist and I regained my speech and vocal abilities. I haven't regained all the feeling in my leg yet, nor did the feeling in my left arm or hand return, but I am grateful that God healed me enough to return to the stage, and

I am miraculously able to sing and entertain once again. Sometimes a person's life has to be broken into pieces before he or she realizes what it means to fully appreciate and understand what life really is about.

For me, God gave me the wakeup call I needed. Even though I may be driven, He showed me just who is in the driver's seat. My life has been blessed beyond anything I could ever have imagined, and I owe it all to Him and Him alone. I was broken and God put me back together.

"In a world filled with hate, we must still dare to hope. In a world filled with anger, we must still dare to comfort. In a world filled with despair, we must still dare to dream. And in a world filled with distrust, we must still dare to believe."
　　　　　　　Michael Jackson, the "King of Pop" – Pop songwriter, artist and singer.

"Uncle Marshall loves you and misses you, Michael, and I know you are looking down from the heavens on me. One day soon we will reunite and sing together in the celestial choir."
　　　　　　　Marshall Thompson, the "Godfather of Pop."

(13)

The day finally arrived. After suffering a life-changing and debilitating stroke, I was going to be back in the spotlight with the lights, the fans, the backstage hustle, and the rush to get to the stage entrance for my post illness debut. These past eight months felt like a whole lifetime, and I missed performing. Then finally, the blissful sound of the ring of the MC's (Master of Ceremonies) microphone announcing my entrance.

　　The MC that night was my good friend, Herb Kent. He and I go way back, to the good old days when the Chi-Town and Motown Soul emerged from the streets of Chicago and Detroit. We were just kids back then, babes in the music business. Now we are, well, let's just say, "well-seasoned." We have been around since the dawn of many genres of music, including Soul, Pop, Rock & Roll; and we've pretty much seen it all.

　　Herb called the Chi-Lites to the stage numerous times in Chicago, but this time was different. This time

I was in a wheelchair, and Frank (Reed) had gone to heaven. Herb and I shared a few words before the concert. He mentioned this book and said he was happy to see me bounce back so quickly, but that he wasn't surprised 'cause that's the kind of guy I am – driven.

This was billed as the Mother's Day 70's Jam at the Arie Crown Theater in Chicago. A group called Bloodstone opened the show followed by the Emotions who really got the crowd "revved up." We followed the Emotions. The Production Manager of the Arie Crown, Shelly Krevitt, was very accommodating and saw that all our needs were met. They were really great, and we appreciated the effort.

I was in the dressing room before the show and all my friends were showering me with love and support. Many visitors stopped by to say hello and show their love; even a young man I met in the hospital who was also confined to a wheelchair stopped by. I never experienced such tremendous support in such a warm way before and that outpouring of love was the motivation for an epic show.

The house was packed. Usually at a venue like the Arie Crown, we do sell out, but it was unusual to pack the house on Mother's day weekend. But holiday or not, we love it when so many folks come out to hear our music. There's just something about 70's Pop music that connects with people's souls and it crosses over so many generations. The audience was full of kids from about 15 – 16 years-old to mom's and pop's that were my age and older just havin' fun.

Then came the call, "Ladies' and gentlemen, let's put our hands together for the Chi-Lites." The audience roared with applause. Even the sound of our drummer's thunderous bass drum couldn't drown out the applause, it was the other way around – praise from the audience engulfed our drummers cadence.

The group sang a few of our hits and the band played as I waited in the wing backstage. I could sense people's curiosity, as they leaned over to one another, "… where's Marshall Thompson," and other's possibly speculating "I wonder if he's too sick to make it to the show," or "… you know that stroke probably put him out of it for good."

When the group finished a few songs, it was time. The music came to a lull. The band members were introduced one by one. Then the announcement came, "The only original member of the legendary Chi-Lites… The Last Man Standing… Mr. Marshall Thompson." The crowd gave me a standing ovation as I entered with assistance to center stage in my wheelchair. The thunderous explosion of applause and clapping with the celebration brought tears to my eyes.

I thanked the audience for their love, and then motioned for the band to start playing. I began by telling my fans that just a few months earlier I couldn't lift my left leg or move my foot. When I picked my left leg up into the air, and gave God the glory, they went wild with excitement.

Looking back in retrospect, I probably should have been a bit more cautious, but I was thinking about my fans and how I felt about them so I motioned to my security to wheel me out on stage and I stood up. That didn't go too well. Mid-way I almost fell, but still I found the strength to hold my own, not for me or because I had to prove something, but to show the people that a medical issue may knock you down, but it doesn't necessarily mean you are knocked out of the ring.

I didn't fall, and I stood there for a minute gazing at the wondrous crowd, and I realized something. What has kept me in the game all these years is not the stage or the lights, or even the attention and accolades I receive. It's not the money either, 'cause Lord knows there's been plenty of dry times. It's not even the fact that music is all I know and is a natural part of my life; many musicians have foundations in music and are native musicians. No, it is the love that I feel from the people who have approached me over the years with stories of how the songs "Oh Girl" or "Have You Seen Her," and "Hot on a Thing" have inspired their love for their spouse, or how the songs even moved their mothers crossing the generational gap. Those are the things that all the fame, money, and instinctive knowledge in music, cannot buy.

After we finished our set, the Stylistics took the stage and closed out what was an incredible show. Having friends like Anthony Argento, Tom Romano, and author, Dane Ladwig come backstage and hang out with me and the boys all night long was uplifting. My wife Tara, was my stronghold that night. Herb Kent and Gene Chandler (the Duke of Earl), and all the other friends who graced the stage that memorable night, truly put a smile in my heart.

After the show at Arie Crown, I headed out to another show in Lisle, Illinois. It's hard to keep a good man down. I know, by the grace of God, and through the love of my friends and fans, I will be bringing Chi-Lites music to the stage for a long time to come, or for as long as God allows, after all, He is the one in control.

We really kicked it in Lisle – tore the house down. Later that night when I was getting ready to settle in for the evening, I thought about how fragile and precious life is. How in a moment all the things that we take for granted, little things like a smile on someone's face, the thump of a baseball hitting the mitt of a child's glove as he or she proudly plays catch with mom or dad, can all change so rapidly. Those special little memories get filed in the back of our minds as our grown up minds become flooded with worry about finances, obligations and other responsibilities.

I think those little memory trinkets in the back of our minds need to come to the forefront every once in a while, and that's why I kid around so much. Sometimes, the hustle and bustle of everyday life needs to be put on hold. Folks need to make time to sit and read a kid a book, or take a child by the hand and go fly a kite with them. Do something, anything, to reflect on what's important in life, 'cause it sure isn't the bills, or the bling, or the social status that adds significance or worth to our existence – and it's essential that the young people realize that.

"And, in the end
The love you take
is equal to the love you make."
— Paul McCartney, The Beatles Illustrated Lyrics

(14)

My wife Tara is my best friend and my refuge. She's also my business manager. She really understands the music industry and the entire business aspect of the Chi-Lites. I lean on her to keep the spokes of the wheel in place and keep it all running smooth. There's no one I trust more than Tara, except God. I could ramble on all day about how important she is to me and the success of my career, but I think it would be better if I let her talk about her experiences.

Well, like Marshall said, I do take care of the business aspect of things, but I am also a backup singer for the Chi-Lites. The best place to start would probably be at the beginning, since that is when my life changed.

In the fall of 1998, when I was a hairdresser at Marshall Fields, I met Ray "Karem" Foreman in the elevator at Fields. I noticed a lanyard around his neck with several laminated tags and I asked what he did for a living. He responded, "I am the road manager for the Chi-Lites. We're getting ready to go on tour in the Bahamas with Boyz II Men, the Stylistics and a whole mess of other bands."

I didn't know much about the Chi-Lites then, but I had a neighbor that lived a few doors down from me who was part of their entourage. I just never took an interest because at that time, I was in my twenties and into the Hip Hop scene.

I said to Karem, "… that sounds fun. I do a little

singing too." He replied, "We're looking for a backup singer. We are going to open auditions when we get back from the Bahamas."

At that time, I was focusing on my hairdressing career and raising two children. My daughter was just a baby and it was important for me not to make rash decisions that would hurt my children, but that also meant not to hold myself back if it would improve my children's future.

Before we parted ways, Karem asked if I knew Marshall Thompson. Looking back, I am kind of embarrassed to say that I responded, "Marshall who?" Then Karem informed me they were getting everyone rounded up to head for the airport to depart for the Bahamas. He gave me his wife's information and said to contact her for an audition. Before he finished giving me the information, Marshall walked onto the elevator and introduced himself. I was a bit self-conscious because I didn't know who he was, but Karem told Marshall that I was going to audition for the backup singing position.

They left for the Bahamas, and I was nervous not knowing the Chi-Lites' music, so I tried to learn as much as I could before they returned. I rarely listened to what we called "old school" music, and, in my mind, the Chi-Lites were as old school as you could get.

The hardest thing was learning what Robert Lester referred to as "trick-harmonies." It's that place where it's so smooth in certain areas it emanates a divine kind of heavenly feeling. Marshall said you had to learn it the right way in order for it to blend with just the perfect touch and sound.

It was a tough learning experience. It might sound simple or you might hear something and just not notice, but the harmonies on the Chi-Lites songs are beautiful beyond words.

When they returned I auditioned for Karem and his wife Diana. I was really surprised when they told me I made it and I was the new backup singer for the Chi-Lites.

My first stage performance with the Chi-Lites was in Atlanta, Georgia, I'll never forget how nervous I was. For some reason, I couldn't explain it at the time, but Marshall had this way of making everyone on the stage feel at ease. We were just having a good time and enjoying the music and the love from the people.

Soon after becoming a backup singer, Marshall asked me if I would like to manage the group. He must have seen something in me that I didn't see. Robert Lester was still with the group, and he taught me a lot. I had to learn about everything from contracts and booking, finances, payroll, setting up travel arrangements and even on stage apparel; and at the end of the day I was responsible for making sure that there was money in the bank account.

It was hard when Marshall wasn't around. I missed him and if he wasn't available to bounce things off of, I had to make split-moment decisions; and it was scary. But that was my job and my life. I had to make sure everybody was happy. Marshall would always say, "It's 10% show business and 90% executive business."

I traveled on the weekends to meet up with the group and make sure everything was running smoothly. It got pretty hectic sometimes, and rest became a luxury.

One of the benefits of managing the group is that I was able to see a side of the business and experience what Marshall went through and it helped me to understand why Marshall is the way he is… why he is filled with so much love and why he is driven.

Many people only see the glamorous side of show business: traveling around the world, the chauffeured limousines, and the adoration and attention. However, they seldom consider the hard work and dedication it takes: negotiating deals, collecting the money from venues, and the many hours of practice it takes to keep the songs tight. When you have an inside perspective, however, you gain a whole new respect for all that's involved.

Marshall and I married on January 16, 2003, and it's vital to have trust when you're married to an entertainer. There are groupies around every corner and you have to be tough, and accept that your spouse, the person you love, is shared with the world. You can never disrespect anyone, no matter how inappropriate the fans or groupies may be, because the fan base makes the entertainer who he/she is.

With Marshall, his generosity extends far beyond our circle of family and friends; he shares his love with the fans. Marshall likes to fix everything and everybody. He does not like so see anyone down, and he refuses to allow anyone to see him down. If it were possible, Marshall would feed the entire world; he's got the biggest heart of anyone I have ever known. Happiness motivates Marshall.

There are few things that get under Marshall's skin, but he despises racial prejudice. Black, white, brown, red, purple, green, it doesn't matter to Marshall. He sees us all as one people, brothers and sisters. He believes in unity and it is that one accord of civilization, of an adoration for life, and for one another, that is reflected throughout the Chi-Lites music.

As Marshall's wife and his manager there is one area, in which I'd like to be more like Marshall. I wish I had a driven spirit like his. Marshall, truly is an inspiration. His life, his music, and his reverence to God through both the bad times and the good is part of what defines him as a true legend. He is my love and my life!

"Such a man as this, with a tenacious spirit to win, who has demonstrated great endurance and stamina, which resulted in many challenges and obstacles throughout his career, Marshall Thompson has emerged victorious in life and on the stage. Truly a man to be admired and revered and I am humbled and privileged to have Marshall as my friend."

Bruce A. Hawes – American singer, pianist, songwriter, and producer. Bruce composed songs for The Spinners, Dionne Warwick, Gladys Knight, R. Kelly, Tupac Shakur, and The Whispers. Bruce also wrote and produced "Where There is Love" for The Whispers, "Dear Ma Ma" for Tupac Shakur, "Sadie" for R. Kelly and "Something On" for legendary artist Melba Moore.

(15)

Being married to Marshall, life is always subject to last minute change so you must be flexible. We are on the go nine to eleven months of the year with tours and shows. Marshall is a very motivated and energetic man so I am never too concerned with his ability to withstand even the most difficult tour schedule.

The only time I witnessed Marshall down or depressed was when we were called out of town to Michael's (Michael Jackson's) home, as a result of his untimely death. On the flight out to Los Angeles (LA) he was very quiet, and that is not his nature, but it was completely understandable, Marshall had known Michael all of Michael's life. The boys (Jackson's) all call Marshall "Uncle Marshall."

As soon as we got to LA, we met up with Katherine and Joe (Jackson family parents). They were very distraught and I felt so sorry for them. Marshall and Joe hugged, cried, talked and tried to comfort one another. We stayed by the Jacksons' for the entire time we were out there. On the day of the Memorial service, we all sat together. At some point, the media interviewed Marshall and Joe and we thought nothing of it. By the time we were on our way home, we heard the news reports coming out about Joe being questioned at Michael's Memorial service, and the media sliced the interview up so badly that they made Joe out to look like something he never was.

Marshall was extremely upset over the loss of Michael and with Joe's interview being ripped apart and his character misrepresented, Marshall grew angrier and more hurt. I was sincerely afraid for Marshall at that point. I had never seen him so distressed. He and his best friend had just gone through a horrendous ordeal, their hearts were in turmoil, and then Joe and the Jackson family were paraded in front of the public and falsely accused of all sorts of dishonesty. There was no compassion for the grieving family. The whole ordeal was horrifying.

Another very challenging and difficult time in our lives occurred recently when Marshall suffered a stroke. We were all excited to tour the Caribbean Islands as members of 2014 Soul Train Tour. We looked forward to getting out of the frigid Chicago winter and replenishing ourselves with some South Seas sunshine.

A few days prior to the tour, however, I sensed something was a little "off." Marshall approached me with a seriousness that was a bit unsettling, and wanted to go over every aspect of the business, including future business plans. "… You need to be prepared, just in case," he told me. That was not like Marshall, he was usually anything but serious. He is always the life of the party, laughing, joking around and having fun.

On the plane, he was still very quiet. When I asked if everything was alright, he said he was "… just a little tired."

As soon as we made it to the cruise ship, Marshall was back to his joking, laughing ways again and I was happy to see the real him return. He met up with other groups and singers, and they reminisced. All was fine until later that afternoon.

Marshall put on a great show, but something was definitely not quite right. He had been sweating profusely, and Marshall never sweat on stage before. During the show it appeared that he was weak, and his movements were not as fluid as they normally were. When he exited the stage, and tried to put his sunglasses on, he was unable to open his hand, but Marshall dismissed his behavior and physical concerns by saying, "I'm just tired. I'll be fine."

We were already down one vocalist, as Frank Reed, our lead singer, was not feeling up to making the trip. He was experiencing illness at the time and it wasn't until later that we learned that Frank would suffer a fatal heart attack and pass away that weekend.

Marshall stood up, went to place his hat upon his head and put on his sunglasses, but again he was having a hard time. It didn't disturb Marshall until he went to pick up his handheld tablet. His tablet is his lifeline to social media and he does not go anywhere without it. This time, he couldn't grasp it and it fell to the floor. I was becoming more frightened by the moment.

Once again, Marshall dismissed it rationalizing that he was weak from the long day, and he was going to take a bath and go to bed. He wanted to sleep. I was sleepless throughout the night, because deep down I felt that Marshall was protecting me from how bad he really felt. Marshall is the kind of guy that keeps things to himself so people won't worry about him.

The next morning we had planned that I would return home to Chicago, while Marshall would continue the tour.

He phoned me, said he went to the ship's infirmary and they determined he was just dehydrated, and gave him some Gatorade to hydrate him. At breakfast that morning Marshall suffered a massive stroke.

Not being there when my husband needed me, was the most helpless feeling I ever experienced. He was rushed to an island medical center on St. Martin. I immediately arranged for his transfer back to Chicago. When he arrived, I was overcome with relief, but I knew this was only the beginning of a long road to recovery. Marshall is the most resilient man I have ever known, but this challenge seemed insurmountable at the time.

Marshall is not the type of man that can be kept down and confined to a bed. As he explained before, he is driven. He survives through the energy he creates from his energetic spirit, and I found a certain security in that thought. Marshall is determined, motivated, and he pushes himself to the limit. I knew that same energy or drive would accelerate his recovery quicker than anything else in the world.

After nearly two months in the hospital, Marshall was ready to come back home. His left leg and arm were still paralyzed, but he was slowly beginning to regain sensation in his leg. From the heyday of Marshall's success, to being in the humbling position of struggling to learn to talk and walk again, is a reflection of just how much one person is capable of if he is an ambassador of God's grace. The "Last Man Standing," is sure to be a tribute to one of the greatest legends of our time – Marshall Thompson.

Last Man Standing

Marshall Thompson 6 years Old

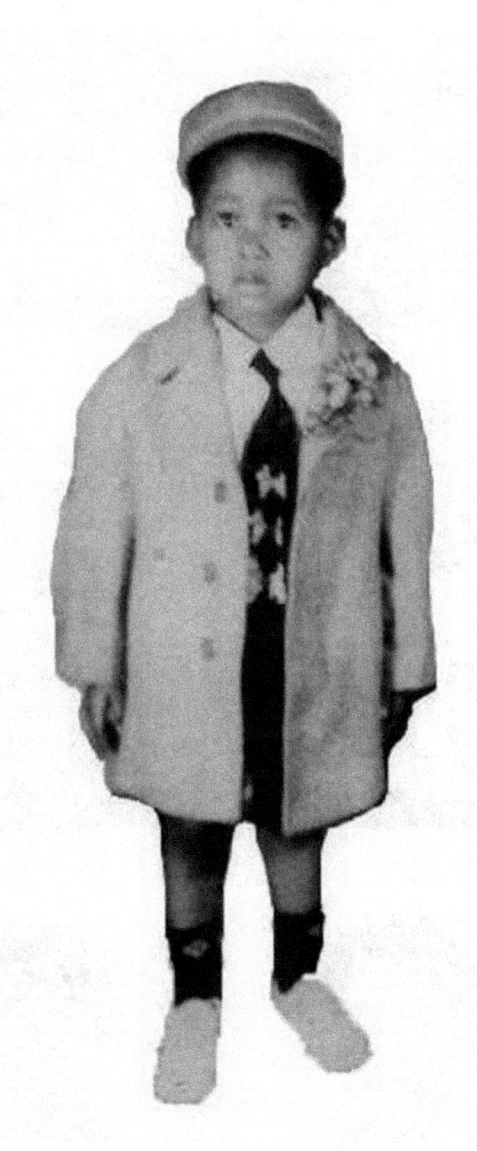

Memories

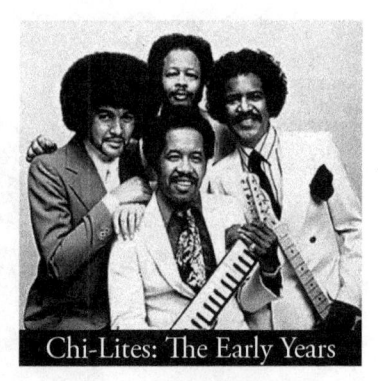

Marshall Thompson

The "Hi-Lites" The early days...

Chi-Lites: The Early Years

Eugene Record

Marshall Thompson

Creadel "Red" Jones

Robert "Squirrel" Lester

Last Man Standing

The Chi-Lites

Chi-Lites and the Dells on Soul Train

Marshall Thompson and British R&B recording sensation Joss Stone

Jermaine Jackson (Jackson 5) and Marshall Thompson

Fantasia and Marshall Thompson

Marshall Thompson and American Idol winner and Grammy Award nominated Ruben Studdard

Marshall romancing the audience

Barry Gordy (Motown) and Marshall Thompson

Last Man Standing

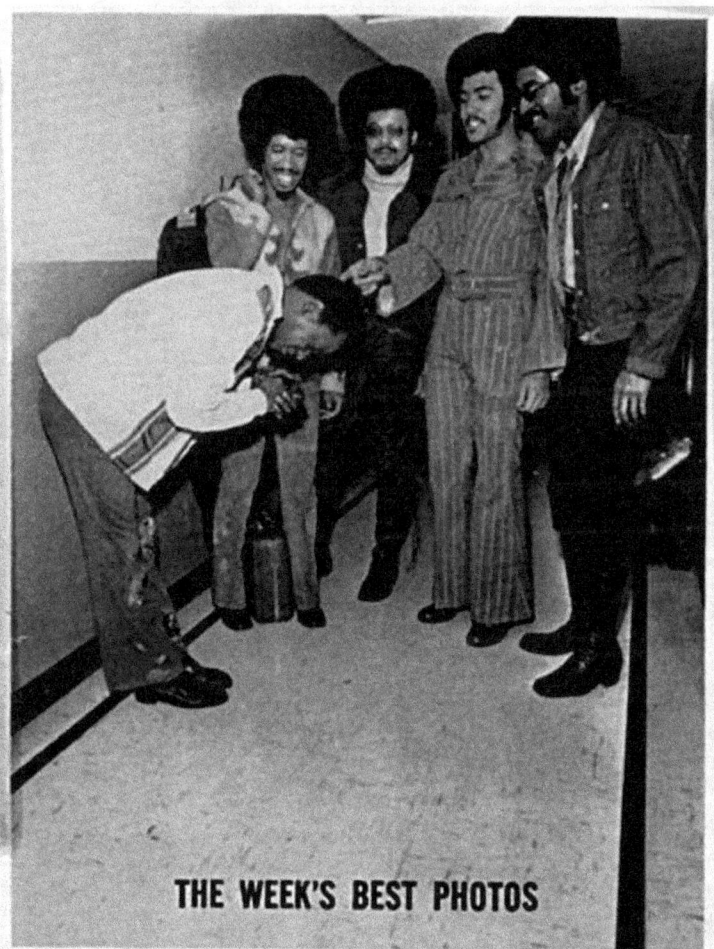

Returning home to Chicago's O'Hare Airport from the UK tour

THE WEEK'S BEST PHOTOS

Jerry Baker

Flip's Homage: Bowing with gratitude, comedian Flip Wilson tells the sensational Chi-Lites that he was more than pleased with their performance on his NBC-TV show. The group sang their solid gold hit, *Have You Seen Her?*

77

Marshall and Tara Thompson

Chi-Lites Preformance Richmond VA. 2003

Tara Thompson

Marshall Takin' care of business!

Marshall Thompson with his step-mother Doris Furbush

Evie and Tanae (Marshall's daughters)

Chi-Lites Band

Richard Steele, Gene Chandler, Herb Kent,
Marshall Thompson, Ken Bedford

First Gold Album

Police Officer Brian Strong,
Marshall Thompson's brother-in-law,
lost his life in 2013 while on duty

Joe Jackson, Rev. Al Sharpton, Marshall Thompson

Marshall Thompson

Joe Jackson, Marshal Thompson, Ne-Yo

A young Justin Timberlake and Marshall Thompson

Chi-Lites and David Copperfield

Marshall Thompson, Clifford Curry, Darryl Payne, King George, DJ Sam Chatman, Eric Bryant

Danielle, Marshall's daughter

Chi-Lites and Bill Wyman (sing, songwriter, bassist) of the Rolling Stones

Billy Brown, Del Payne, Al Goodman

Chi-Lites Dancers

Comedian Kym Whitley

Del Brown

Bruce Swedien, Chi-Lites Recording Engineer

BB King and Marshall Thompson

Chi-Lite and Elton John in the UK 1974

Ginini Thompson (Marshall's daughter) and Marshall Thompson

Sandie, Marshall's daughter

Marshall Thompson's children

Gene Chandler, Jerry Butler, Marshall Thompson

Joe "Jobie" Thomas (Enchantments), Emanuel "EJ" Johnson (Enchantments), Gerald Alston (Manhattans), Marshall Thompson, Winfred "Blue" Lovett (Manhattans), Willie Albert "Al" Goodman (Ray, Goodman & Brown) (l-r)

Last Man Standing

Chi-Lites Road Manager, Dazy Brown

Publicity Agent Larissa Tyler

The Biggest record we ever had (Oh Girl) sold 3 Million copies in 1972

Marshall's children (l-r), Mar-shell, Darnell, Craig

Marshall Thompsons Mothers sister (Alena Reed) 104-years-old, surrounded by Marshall's children

Constance "Connie" Thompson

Constance Thompson

Reggie Thomas the Chi-Lites 1st manager in 1965

Jack Bart, the Chi-Lites manager for the past 30 years.

My Chicago Guy's, Tom Romano, Dane Ladwig, Anthony Argento (l-r)

U.C. FIELDHOUSE
SAT. MAY 24

KOOL & the GANG
"SPIRIT OF BOOGIE"

"TOBY" The "YOU GOT TO BE THE ONE"
CHI-LITES
"GIVE MORE POWER TO THE PEOPLE"

MAJOR HARRIS
"LOVE WON'T LET ME WAIT"

Admission:
$6.00 ADVANCE
$6.50 Day of Show

Ticket Locations: SHILLITOS..
All SEARS ROEBUCK Stores
Plus.. CALLOWAYS
and STAGS BARBER SHOPS

Promoters: A WALKER AND SEARS PRODUCTION

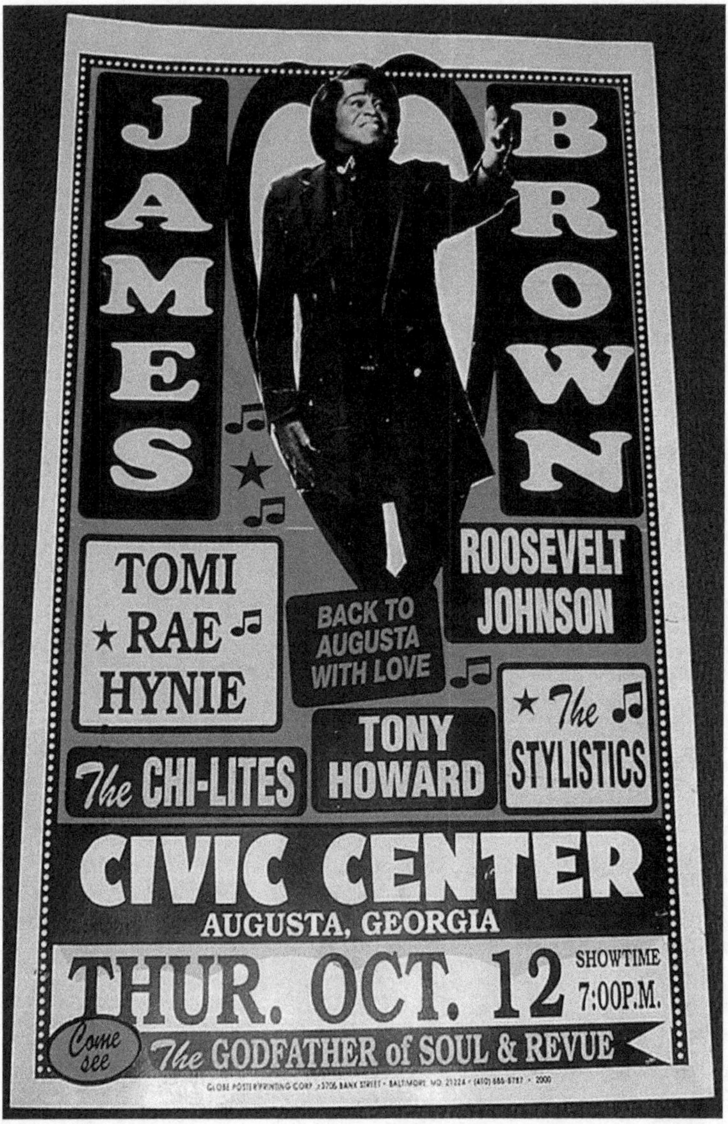
JAMES
BROWN
TOMI RAE HYNIE
BACK TO AUGUSTA WITH LOVE
ROOSEVELT JOHNSON
The STYLISTICS
The CHI-LITES
TONY HOWARD
CIVIC CENTER
AUGUSTA, GEORGIA
THUR. OCT. 12
SHOWTIME 7:00P.M.
Come see
The GODFATHER of SOUL & REVUE

Carl Davis

Robert "Squirrel" Lester

Chi-Lites 2014 at the Nokia Theater in LA.

GENEALOGY & ROOTS

THE LEGENDARY CHI-LITES AND THE CHI-TOWN SOUND

BY DANE LADWIG – AUTHOR

THE ORIGIN OF POP MUSIC

The history of music is rich with cultural and spiritual beliefs. Past and present, music has defined societies and shaped values. Primitive music embraced nature's sounds and rhythms. When musical instruments were introduced (according to *Easton's Bible Dictionary*) around 3600 BC, harmonies and rhythms began to take on a refined sophistication and a "heartbeat" that compelled the listener to interact on an emotional level.

Roots of music speaks not only of the origin of music, but to the emotion and sensation that has evolved with music. Composition and harmonies, as we have come to know them today, whether classical, country, Rock and Roll, R&B, Pop, etc., can all be traced back to a culture, and a society of the past that innovated and transformed a sound enjoyed much in the same way we modernize music we hear today.

As we have progressed through time, music has evolved and lead us into new horizons. Revolution and reform in civilization, and its global influence, has introduced rebellion and an unrest, which resulted in a revolution of new innovative concepts and philosophies in music. With every significant transitional time in history, a keynote shift in music can be traced to those noteworthy events. When the acceptable music composition once mandated that elegant sophistication necessitated that the listener find favor in a particular artist to gain social acceptance; today, music has crossed the boundaries that once separated the social classes, and refinement holds no control over music.

As we observe the transitions in music, specifically those associated with the Chi-Lites, we can notice several innovations that were instrumental in the success of Pop music. Individuals like the Chi-Lites revolted against socially accepted ideals and used their music to influence history. These innovators were forerunners in establishing a new world order, forging the way for a new sound that Baby Boomers craved. It started back in the 1930's with the influence of Big Bands and Swing music.

At that time we were introduced to recording, and for the first time in history you could listen to music on one side of the planet while the band was playing a concert hall on the other side of the globe. Following WWII, the troops found a sense of solace and comfort listening to ballads on the "long playing disc" or what we came to know as the "LP." With the advances and sound improvement in LP's, recording companies were able to manufacture low-cost records that anyone could afford, and by the 50's, recording studios were introducing new talent and raking in big bucks on a daily basis.[1]

With the introduction of new standards in recording, the artist was limited only by his or her imagination. Stereo recordings opened the floodgates for recording artists and producers as well. Electronic guitars and overdubbing were the new rage and the more you experimented with the sound, the more success you were likely to obtain. Innovation and inspiration were the keys to success. With top record labels such as RCA, Capitol, Columbia, Dot, Electra, and Phillips, just to mention a handful of the conglomerates, only someone void of common sense would go head-to-head with these recording company industrialists thinking they could attain victory on an Independent label. Many would say it is, "a fool's deed!"

In 1952, radio DJ Allen Freed took the radio audience to new heights with his show, *Moondog's Rock & Roll Party*. Freed, the first ever Rock & Roll DJ, and concert promoter, realized that young kids were buying

R&B records at the local record store. That is when the light bulb went off in Freed's head to "cash in." Caucasian youth bought every R&B record on the rack, but Freed did not want to promote his show as an R&B program; the 50's were still riddled with prejudice and Freed recognized this, so he named his show, *Moondog's Rock and Roll Party*, hence the origin of "Rock and Roll."

In 1957 Freed and all of America experienced the backlash of America's predisposition to bigotry and discrimination when Freed was given his own program on ABC-TV and his then nationwide televised Rock & Roll show, which featured Frankie Lymon dancing with a white girl. The viewing audience was outraged. Freed's problems only escalated when in 1958, at the Boston Arena, Freed was charged with "Incitement to Riot" and accusation that his Rock & Roll show was "overly exuberant."

With this new Rock & Roll rage, many budding musicians, both black and white, were questioning decisions about which direction to take their music. Buddy Holly and the Crickets was a Country-Gospel group that shifted gears to Rock & Roll. Elvis Presley, one of the most significant music related icons of the twentieth-century, originally sang country and gospel music. Then there were the R&B artists who dedicated a lifetime to the Blues, and rightly so; Blues flowed through their veins.

In the 30's, if you took a walk down the streets of Chicago, Baltimore, Cincinnati, Detroit, Newark, New Jersey, Philadelphia, San Francisco or Washington D.C., you were sure to hear the neighborhood "group" harmonizing. A decade later, in the 40's, Doo Wop originated in African American communities, but by the late 50's it had gained mainstream popularity and was all the rage. It was not uncommon to see white kids hanging out and attempting to emulate their favorite Doo Wop groups.

Doo Wop, a vocal based R&B style, actually took shape with Bill Kenny of the Ink Spots in the 1930's. Kenny, known as "The Godfather of Doo Wop," created a unique sound by featuring a high tenor lead and in the middle of the song a peculiar, but very pleasing and rhythmic "talking bass" would carry the heartbeat of the tune. This would come to be known as the "top and bottom" format.

The senseless syllables, little to no instrumentation, simple music and lyrics, and a straightforward uncomplicated beat, accented with precision harmonies, offered the artists an abundance of options, and the listener a pure unexplainable and all-encompassing sound. As vocal groups were challenged to come up with new material, the Doo Wop scene exploded with possibilities never before imagined. The decay that had once stifled growth in American values had now started to experience the evolution and rebellion of independence and youth.

The Truth Behind the Rage
(The Black Panther Movement)

With the 60's movement towards democratic values, minorities and youth had set the bar for the female population to fight for equality. With the erosion of black communities caused by segregation, poverty and unemployment, there was little choice but to address the issues at hand vigorously. Through sit-ins, freedom rides, and protest marches, the African-American community sent a message of intolerance of injustice toward an entire race. Their message of independence rang loud and clear through Doo Wop, R&B, and Soul music.

America was transforming and her people and their music would be forced to evolve with the times. The Vietnam War forced America to examine her resilience and world power. A symbolic gesture echoing America's unrest was demonstrated in 1969 in the Catskills, New York, when 32 bands and more than 400,000 youth gathered to celebrate a harmonious unification of love and peace. The Woodstock Festival, as it was branded, was a three day music festival that characterized yet another revolution and transformation in music history, one that emerged at a time when America was near ruin.

What led up to this pivotal transformation began in the late 1950's. As music was on the cusp of, perhaps its most significant reform, a group from the south side of Chicago emerged as innovators and visionaries that made the world, and the music industry, take notice. With a song titled, "(For God's Sake) Give More Power to the People (1971)," written by Eugene Record of the Chi-Lites, it became clear that when the militant gang, the Black Panthers, adopted the song as their motto, this hard-driving song would serve as the tip of the iceberg of the Chi-Lites' involvement with the radical Black Panther movement.

The slogan for the Black Panther party became a cornerstone of the turbulent 70's Civil Rights movement, and the pumped fists of black righteousness that accompanied the "Power to the People" slogan, in the face of opposition, was seen as a threat. Black Panther activists were allies to no one, and many times, they were depicted in black swat and/or military gear brandishing high-powered, automatic weapons.

Affirmation by the Black Panther Nationalists group of the "Black Power" message was echoed when the Chi-Lites leader, Marshall Thompson, admitted publicly that they had received "protection" from the Black Panther Party and that they played at many Black Panther rallies. Disturbing as that may be, the Chi-Lites became even more c0ntroversail when they embraced a radical ideology that promoted one race as a dominant ethnic group over all others. The Black Panther's teachings stated that the Black plight was not only to rise above oppression, but to use violence or any means necessary, to ensure that the Black movement succeeded and remained at the top of their game.

THE CHI-LITES

DEMISE OF MOTOWN – CORKY "THE GALOOT" – THE MOB CONNECTION – RICO – RISE OF THE "CHI-SOUND"

In the 1960s, Brunswick Records rebuilt an empire. In the 40s when Brunswick retired, Decca purchased the company as a subsidiary of Decca, Brunswick began releasing all new talent in the R&B arena. In the 50s, Brunswick became a leader in Rock & Roll and was signing acts such as Buddy Holly and the Crickets, and subsequently they were back on top, leading the industry in recording sales, in producing, and showcasing new talent.

Brunswick's Executive Vice-President, Nat Tarnapol, managed: Jackie Wilson, the Chi-Lites, Tyrone Davis, Barbara Acklin, the Young-Holt Unlimited, Gene Chandler, Otis Leavill, the Lost Generation, Walter Jackson, Erma Franklin, Hamilton Bohannon, Lavern Baker, and Little Richard. When Carl Davis, the label's producer, from the Chicago based Brunswick operation, joined Brunswick in the mid-60s, Davis strictly produced R&B music, while Nat concentrated on Rock & Roll and R&B. Nat Tarnapol, however, eventually ended up with a 50% interest in Brunswick Records.

In 1960, the hottest name in the entertainment business was not Elvis Presley; it was Jackie Wilson and his manager, Nat Tarnapol. Acting on behalf of Wilson, Tarnapol accomplished the unbelievable; he convinced Decca Records, a subsidiary of Brunswick Records, to sign Jackie Wilson (and Nat Tarnapol) for $250,000.00, with the additional stipulation that Brunswick could become an independent label (of course with Nat Tarnapol as a 50% stockholder. This amount was six times the money that Elvis Presley and Sun Records received from RCA just four years prior.

Wilson was expected to turn out a stellar money-making album. Carl Davis of Brunswick's Chicago based operation produced the album, but it was not met with the success they had hoped for. Decca, facing its own financial woes, became a subsidiary of MCA, Brunswick; and Nat Tarnapol moved and purchased the remaining rights to Brunswick.

Brunswick and Tarnapol were under government surveillance for many years, as foul play with the record rights and the royalties, as well as the taxes owed to the IRS, were in question. The scandal led to an indictment and it was much more than Tarnapol could endure. Carl Davis of Chi-Sound Records was handling most of Tarnapol's recording contracts out of Chicago at the time.

Paul Tarnapol, Carl Davis, and Brunswick Records were now sitting ducks. It was obvious that the FBI was after more than just the financial records of the recording artists and the record companies. The FBI indictment in the Grand Jury Investigation that specifically named Nat Tarnapol, and Marshall Thompson of the Chi-Lites, in addition to Brunswick Records, sought the corporate records "… for the specific purpose of proving causality," were according to the FBI indictment, "inconclusive." For that reason, all charges were dropped.

Nevertheless, the FBI succeeded in accomplishing its goal. Their main objective was to gain access to Brunswick's (and Tarnapol's, Thompson's, and the Chi-Lites') business records in order to build a case against: Morris Levy a.k.a. "the Godfather of Music;" reputed mobster, Dominic Canterino of New York's Genovese crime family; Vincent (the Chin) Gigante; and lastly, Gaetano (Tommy) Vastola.

Vastola, also known as Corky, Sonny, the Gallot, and

the Big Guy; a reputed mobster of the (Carlo) Gambino family, and former cellmate of John Gotti. He was Carl Davis's right hand man and the booking/business manager of the Chi-Lites, Jackie Wilson, and many other well-known artists. The FBI was attempting to cripple organized crime through the music industry. The most successful way to achieve that goal and effectively take down the mob was through the Racketeer Influenced and Corrupt Organizations Act (RICO).

RICO is a law that, simply put, focuses on racketeering. It is specifically designed to grant extended criminal penalties, and civil cause of action for acts of organized crime. In short, the leaders of organized crime - crime bosses and heads of family - can be tried for crimes they ordered or assisted others with. There are steep penalties associated with RICO infractions including monetary fines, and imprisonment up to 20 years depending on the severity of the infraction. In addition, in RICO incidents, the individual's personal and business property, is forfeited and seized by the U.S. government, and they can also be held liable for damages of up to, but not to exceed, 3 times the amount of damages related to the offense[2].

Following several years of undercover investigation, it was learned that Brunswick Records and its subsidiaries were tied to organized crime, and many (if not all) of the musicians connected to Brunswick (and Motown) and its subsidiaries were also tied to organized crime. In all, 19 Brunswick executives were indicted on charges of mail fraud and tax evasion. Nat Tarnapol, manager of the Chi-Lites, Jackie Wilson, and other great performers, was additionally charged with extorting millions of dollars in royalties from the acts he managed[3].

Many of Jackie Wilson's fans felt that the financial collapse Mr. Wilson experienced as a result of Brunswick's and Nat Tarnapol's underhanded schemes to defraud Mr. Wilson out of his life's earnings, was directly related to his impending death. During the prolonged period of the trial, Jackie Wilson suffered a heart attack on national television. While singing "*Lonely Teardrops,*" on Dick Clark's Good Old Rock & Roll Review, as he sang the lyric… "My heart is cryin', cryin'," Jackie Wilson's lifeless body crumpled on the stage. He was said to have "no apparent heartbeat" when the paramedics arrived. He was revived at the hospital, after enduring 30 minutes without a pulse or a heartbeat, and the lack of oxygen to his brain, he then slipped into a coma.

Eventually, Jackie Wilson was released from the hospital; and placed in a residential care center, the Medford Leas Retirement Center in Medford, NJ. A few years later, Jackie Wilson passed away, and was buried at Westlawn Cemetery near Detroit[4] in an unmarked pauper's grave, reserved for indigents and people who have no money.

How does Jackie Wilson and his possible ties to organized crime, connect to the Chi-Lites? For starters, they shared the same business manager, Nat Tarnapol and there are also much deeper "ties" to organized crime. Tommy James, of Tommy James and the Shondells, tells all in his book, *Me, the Mob, and the Music: One Helluva Ride with Tommy James & The Shondells* (2011), and he gives a chilling account of how the music industry's magnates and big kahunas, drove the music industry to its demise.

According to Tommy James, the music mogul and reputed gangster, Morris Levy gave Alan "Moondog" Freed his start in music as a DJ. Freed became a target of Levy. Morris Levy managed Frankie Lymon and the Teenagers, and bilked them out of a fortune from the recording rights because of the number of records sold and the numerous recordings of "Why Do Fools Fall in Love?" Many remakes by other entertainers added to Morris Levy's fortune. Levy got "filthy rich" off the creative efforts, and the naivety, of young entertainers.

If you recall, Morris Levy was Nat Tarnapol's boss, and Nat Tarnapol managed both Jackie Wilson and the Chi-Lites. In Tommy James' memoirs further stated that not a move was made in the music industry without a stamp of approval from Morris Levy, and every deal that was made profited Levy and placed the artists further in his debt. At one point, Tommy James tried to hire lawyers to protect and recoup his financial and royalty interests that were held by Morris Levy, but he stated, "All the lawyers I hired were either bought off or scared off[5]." Levy swindled Tommy James and the Shondells out of more than 30 million dollars[6].

If it sounds like something out of the movie the Godfather, or Casino, that's because it was; only the commodity was not bootleg alcohol, cocaine, or guns, it was artistic royalties, from which there was a ton of money to be made. It seemed that Morris Levy was the strong-arm and the benefactor. John Lennon was also in a heated battle with Levy over the rights to his mega-hit, "Come Together" and Levy made it clear that Lennon would not win the war, by issuing intimidating verbal threats to Lennon. While the legal battle was going on, Mark David Chapman gunned down John Lennon. Many felt Levy was the culprit behind Chapman's so-called motive, but Chapman gave a mocked-up story involving his dismay over lyrics to Lennon's song "Imagine[7]."

As "mobbed-up" as the recording industry was, one thing was certain; artists such as the Chi-Lites, who wanted to make a name for themselves, had no choice but to follow the leadership of organized crime. Although the Chi-Lites manager was Nat Tarnapol, and his Executive

Manager was Morris Levy, Levy had to answer to syndicate boss Soldato "Sonny" (Tommy) Gaetano Vastola of the Decavalcante mob family of New Jersey. Naturally, the "Big Guy" as Vastola was known by in the industry, would report to his bosses, one of the Caporegime, and they to the Consigliere, then it would reach the Underboss, and if it went as high as the family Boss, that pretty much meant that heads were about to roll.

The truth of the matter is this vocal group of four black singers, the Chi-Lites, did not make enemies amongst the Jew (Levy) or the Italians. Nonetheless, it took its toll on the group's dynamics. Although the upheaval was masked as one member leaving and being replaced by another, the truth is that members resigned because they were rebelling against conforming to a life of servitude in which the lucrative business of performing and composing hit records meant little to no financial compensation for the musicians!

Through the test of time, Marshall Thompson's determination to carry on the legacy of the remnant he once created had put him in the poor house. Although he appears to be so proud of his creation that he would never admit it, Mr. Thompson's decision to shine a proverbial light of prosperity and harmony on the Chi-Lites, although virtuous, has left him near penniless.

Between the financial disparities the Feds exposed in the Grand Jury Indictment (in excess of 1.5 million dollars), and the royalty issues the Chi-Lites faced with Nat Tarnapol, and the financial and legal struggles amongst the group members over royalties and rights, the group had, and has, been in shackles since they first hit the big time. The Chi-Lites hit an all-time high in the late 60s to early 70s, the bottom has been falling out ever since.

Tommy's "Boys"

(Exclusive Interview with Convicted Mobster – Gaetano "Tommy" Vastola)

I had the opportunity to interview Tommy Vastola. I expected to talk to a hard-nosed, tough gangster who had seen enough to write the book on organized crime. I was nervous at first, but a minute into the call that nervousness left and was replaced by conversation with a seasoned man who had paid his debt to society and since put his priorities in order with a sense of morality intact.

This phone interview was a big deal as Tommy Vastola had not discussed his days with Brunswick Records, or his incarceration as a result of the Federal Rico indictment, since he was sentenced to 20 years on 09/19/86. In 1989 Vastola and New York crime boss, John Gotti shared a cell at Metropolitan Federal Correction's facility located in Manhattan and while incarcerated, they learned that they were once again facing criminal racketeering charges.

"Dapper Don" as Gotti was often referred to, felt that Vastola and he had a few too many personal conversations and that the Fed's were going to flip (turn them into informants/witnesses for prosecution) Vastola and offer him a deal if he would turn State's evidence. Mr. Gotti ordered an immediate hit on the DeCalvalcante soldier – Vastola. Hits on other family members were viewed as a direct attack of the family, and a mob war was about to break out.

To make matters worse, members of the DeCalvalcante family were recruited by Gotti in the plot to kill Vastola, as were members of the Genovese crime family[8]. The Fed's needed to act quickly to protect the safety of Tommy Vastola, and they did. On July 14, 1992 crime boss of the Gambino family, John Gotti; Giovanni Riggi, the DeCavalcante family boss; John D'Amato an underboss; and Bartolomeo Nicholo, identified as an associate of the Genovese crime family, were all sentenced on charges of conspiracy to murder. They were bugged and tapped; and recorded conversations of the plot to "hit" Vastola led to their convictions. Coincidentally, Bartolomeo Nicholo was said to have been Tommy Vastola's closest friend and confidant at the time of the conviction.

Tommy Vistola, once having a price on his head, was either scared of the fact that his life was near the end, or he was a true outfit man who, until now, has never uttered a word of his dealings with organized crime. Then again, what does he have to fear? The people that wanted him erased have all expired.

Subsequently his concerns of the day seemed to shift, from the dirty deeds of the mob scene of his youth, to his grandchildren. He bragged about his grandson's hockey skills, the financial strain associated with being a dedicated hockey family, and the pressures of constant travel connected to being a sports minded family dedicated to supporting their children's dreams.

Within minutes our conversation returned to a serious discussion. Tommy said, "As far as my boys are concerned, you can ask me anything. I was with the Chi-Lites from the very beginning and I was there 'til the very end." I clarified who his "boys" were, and he named each Chi-Lite by name. "I got them on the Flip Wilson show and that's what made their careers," he said with an obvious sense of pride. Tommy Vastola, then explained his relationship with Brunswick, and his dealings with Nat Tarnapol, Johnny Roberts, and Morris Levy. He inferred they were "bad people," who took advantage of everyone. On more than one occasion, as if I would forget, he frequently reminded me, "You know that shit that went down… RICO and all. That was all BS [Bullshit]. I was set-up. The Fed's knew I was clean, but they wanted me."

I knew that if I pressed him on the RICO case, his incarceration, or being locked up in the same cell with New York crime boss, John Gotti, he would fold, so I suggested a follow up call, which he agreed to.

Thirty-six hours later, I called Tommy Vastola to continue where we left off. I was stunned by the polar-opposite of this conversation compared to the first. In true gangster style, Mr. Vastola lawyered up. He said, "I'll discuss this with you but only if you fly out here to New Jersey and sit with me and my lawyer."

Perhaps it was the result of the many gangster movies I had watched over the years, but what I envisioned was far from a sit down dinner meeting and chatting over old-times. I declined the invitation and thanked Mr. Vastola for his time. I did wonder though, what might have taken place in the last 36 hours to change his heart. After all, he did say the Chi-Lites were his "boys" and that he would do anything for them. Maybe anything except implicate himself in any questionable activities associated with Brunswick.

THE TRUTH ABOUT THE EARLY YEARS AND BEYOND

In the late 1950s, the Chanteurs, consisting of Eugene "Gene" Record, Robert "Squirrel" Lester, and Clarence Johnson merged bands with Marshal Thompson and Creadel "Red" Jones of the Desideros and they christened the new vocal group the "Hi-lites." In 1964 the group decided to pay tribute to their hometown turf by adding a "C" and retitled the group "Marshall and the Chi-Lites." Soon after, they shortened the name to the "Chi-Lites." Many speculate that the origin of Chicago's famed nickname "Chi-Town" came about in the 70's and that it originated in the African-American communities. In fact, it was coined as it was introduced by the Chi-Lites on stage in the 60's, and it caught on like wildfire with fans, and soon became a moniker that would be associated with the Windy City.

The music associated with Chicago in the 50's through the 60's was not the Pop soul and smooth sounds of the Chi-Lites, but it was more the tenaciously gritty urban blues and the heart wrenching, driven R&B. That lush, velvety sound that is hallmark for the Chicago based Chi-Lites, along with four-part harmonies and layered inventions, soothed listener's ears with the warm pleading tenor and falsetto driven scores. From passionate ballads to protest songs, the Chi-Lites' compositions impacted their listeners through difficult and shifting times; that is why the Chi-Lites music has lived on for five decades and lost little in its message over a half-century.

Gene Record was the group's primary songwriter, however, the other members collaborated as well, and other musical talent such as Barbara Acklin, and others, often co-wrote songs with the Chi-Lites. Marshall Thompson was the driving force that held everything together and made sure that the group got bookings and were paid for their shows. Many attribute the success of the Chi-Lites to the management of Marshall Thompson.

Every member of the Chi-Lites was musically inclined and educated with degrees and/or professionally trained in music. Gene Record played rhythm guitar and Congo's; Red was also skilled on the Congo's; Squirrel often times sustained the beat by way of percussion instruments, most often the tambourine; and Marshall was an accomplished drummer by the age of five, who also played the harmonica and the Melodica (used on "Oh Girl".) Each member also had voice training lessons; and to assist in the harmonic balance and blending, they specialized in jazz scat singing. Scat singing is a challenging skill that necessitates singers to sing improvised melodies and rhythms using their voice as an instrument rather than a dialogue or speaking vehicle.

The Chi-Lites signed with Chicago based Brunswick Records in 1968. One year later, they topped the charts (number 10) in R&B with their hit record "Give It Away." Although they had minor success with "Let Me Be The Man Daddy Was" they could not claim another chart climbing record until early '71 when they released, "Are You My Woman? (Tell Me So)." In '71 when they released "(For God's Sake) Give More Power to the People," they were recognized on the Pop charts, and what ensued subsequently set the stage for even greater popularity and fame. The time came to turn the music toward a different direction. Soulful ballads became the songs the Chi-Lites embraced that forever earned them a position of legendary status.

In 1971 and 1972, the Chi-Lites held major back-to-back hits with, "Have You Seen Her," and "Oh Girl." These are the songs that revolutionized Pop music and became the principal focus of many vocal groups attention. To capture the sounds and the harmonies that the Chi-Lites did so well, and so effortlessly, inspired every musician and vocalist to "up" their game.

They were not met with the same success on subsequent productions, however, they were turning out some very big transatlantic smash records in R&B including: "Stoned Out of My Mind;" "Homely Girl;" "There Will Never Be Any Peace (Until God Is Seated at the Conference Table);" and "Toby," four singles which all ranked on the top ten R&B list.

Many personnel changes ensued with the Chi-Lites as the group's involvement with Brunswick Records began to disintegrate, as did the careers of the Chi-Lites (see the *Member Chronology* at the end of this chapter). Brunswick met with serious financial troubles, and as a result, the producers at Brunswick were no longer able to promote the Chi-Lites records. As news of Brunswick's deteriorating financial status began a decline in the infrastructure of Brunswick Records, the Internal Revenue Service filed charges against the Chi-Lites for tax evasion (1972 -1976 unpaid taxes). The Chi-Lites settled the matter in court, and repaid the IRS, however, it took a toll on the once prosperous group's finances, and skewed the public view of the Chi-Lites. This event would all but end the reign of popularity, along with the hit producing Chi-Lites emotional and expressive ballads once fashioned from adolescent experiences of innocence and worldly naiveties. Their once spotless reputation had become tarnished by the excessive greed of the entertainment business.

Eugene Record, the bands "word man" who spent

the past twenty-years writing Chi-Lites music abandoned the band. Gene was replaced by David Scott and Danny Johnson, and instead spent time recording as a solo artist, unable to make a mark in the industry without the distinguished vocal melodies once recognized as that great Chi-Lites silk-as-honey synchronized harmony. A few short years later, in 1980, realizing that the magic of the Chi-Lites was a joint effort, not a solo one, all the original members reformed and began cutting records again on the "Chi-Sound" label.

In 1982, "Hot on a Thing Called Love" jumped up the national charts to number 18. A year later, Creadel "Red" Jones was asked to leave the Chi-Lites due to his ongoing and increasingly perilous drug dependency issues. The Chi-Lites joined LARC Records, and although they produced records, they did not make a mark on the charts. In 1990, the group fractured and the lead singer, Eugene Record left and was replaced by Anthony Watson and Frank Reed. Four years later, Creadel "Red" Jones passed away.

July 26, 1997, was the day that changed history forever and tested the strength of the longstanding Chi-Lites. It was a beautiful sunny 70° day on the drive back to Chicago from a concert in Pennsylvania. Around 7:00 AM, on the westbound lane of Interstate 80, about 55 miles north of Pittsburgh, the vehicle the Chi-Lites were traveling in hit an embankment. Both Frank Reed and Marshall's wife, Constance Thompson were ejected from the car. Frank Reed survived, however, he was listed in critical condition requiring emergency surgery and insertion of a metal plate in his spine. Constance, the backbone of the Chi-Lites, did not survive; she died.

Marshall was absolutely devastated. There were more than 5,000 people who attended Constance Thompson's memorial service including dignitaries, entertainers, and fans of the Chi-Lites. Although Marshall's spirits were lifted temporarily by the turnout of his wife's service, the anguish was apparent on his grief-ridden face.

Constance managed the group and their finances, and with her absence, the future of the Chi-Lites was beginning to look very bleak. A year later, the group released a new album *Help Wanted,* and the title song was dedicated to the memory of Constance, "Hold Onto Your Dreams." Although the album did not make it on the charts, the single dedicated to Constance made the top 100 list in R&B at position 93. In 2000, the Chi-Lites were inducted into the R&B Foundation.

Another crushing blow tested the loyalty of Chi-Lites fans in 2001, when the one member with a record for longevity and stability, Marshall Thompson, creator of the Chi-Lites, who stood as a pillar of their firm position in the Pop music scene, was sentenced to prison. Thompson was indicted on charges stemming from an FBI sting involving police officers selling badges.

Formerly sworn to "protect and serve," Marshall Thompson, serving as a police officer in the town of Maywood Park Police District, was charged with selling badges to "donors" and transferring funds as a "bag man." The badges were sold to anyone who would pay the steep price of $2500.00 for the privilege to carry a weapon in public, or display a badge, and for other "perks" as part of the status that went along with being recognized as a cop.

Marshall was working as a fundraiser for the Maywood Park Police District, raising money to buy uniforms, and police equipment. He had a lot of success in this area, largely due to his status as a celebrity, and notoriety as a Chi-Lite. Donors were contacting Marshall and offering donations to suburban Dixmoor Park District Police

Department, and Marshall accepted, allegedly stating that he never realized that Dixmoor Police Chief, James Parks, was extorting very large sums of money from the donors.

Marshall Thompson did not handle the funds, etc., he steered the donors to Dixmoor, and in turn, Chief Parks was extorting the money. However, Marshall agreed to plead guilty in return for his testimony against the Dixmoor Police Chief. His guilty plea earned him one year in Oxford Correctional Institution in Oxford, Wisconsin.

Four years passed and in 2005, news reached Marshall Thompson that Eugene "Gene" Record, died at the age of 64 following a long bout with cancer. A deep sadness engulfed the remaining Chi-Lites. They lost their good friend, Gene, and could not share in the exciting news that the Chi-Lites were inducted into the Vocal Group Hall of Fame, an event that had become bittersweet. In 2010, Robert "Squirrel" Lester succumbed to cancer (liver) leaving the group of founding members diminished to one solitary living member – Marshall Thompson.

Through the years, there were many replacement members in the Chi-Lites, and the argument was made that if you closed your eyes you could not distinguish the difference between the "stand ins" and the originals. However, the enchanting melodies and magical compositions that are the cornerstone of the Chicago based group, could only be enjoyed at their finest when the original members chanted their rhythmic verses themselves, with the passion they envisaged when they initially composed the scores.

Marshall Thompson, the "rock" that founded the Chi-Lites, was now the last enduring legendary Chi-Lite, and as the saying goes, "time keeps on tickin'." In February of 2014, while on the Soul Train Caribbean Cruise Tour, Marshall received word that his longtime friend and co-member of the Chi-Lites, Frank Reed (who replaced Eugene Record in 1990) had suffered a fatal heart attack. Marshall was set to entertain on the main stage and kept the news about Frank bottled up, but clearly it took its toll on Thompson.

Marshall Thompson had experienced an embolic stroke. He was transferred from the Bahamas to a hospital in the states and was listed in critical condition. Marshall was now in the most challenging fight of his life. The left side of his body was completely paralyzed and his speech was impaired. With the last remaining Chi-Lite declining in health it seemed inevitable the Chi-Lites' legacy was facing extinction.

After four months of intensive in-patient rehabilitation, however, Marshall Thompson's determined attitude and hard work miraculously paid off. He was released from rehab having made remarkable strides regaining his speech, the use of his leg, and partial use of his arm. Amazingly on May 10, 2014, Marshall Thompson returned to the stage at the Arie Crown Theater in Chicago, IL. As he was rolled out onto the stage in his wheelchair, the enthusiastic crowd made it clear that the Chi-Lites had not missed a beat, and that an abundance of love and loyalty was reserved for the magical moment when Marshall returned to the stage. As he took the microphone, he thanked God, and his fans, and also addressed the former members of the Chi-Lites, "… Sorry my friends, he stated [as he pointed to the ceiling of the auditorium], I miss you all, but I just ain't ready to leave yet!" Then he placed his hand upon his heart.

"RED" JONES AND THOMPSON: NATURAL DEATH OR ?

In August of 1994, the Glendale California City Hall employees, discovered that the aged and crumpled, homeless man residing on the crescent-shaped concrete bench, beside the illuminated bronze globe adorning the City Hall lawn, would no longer be lining up shopping carts to protect his earthly possessions.

The homeless man, "Red" Creadel Jones, left the Chi-Lites for the last time in 1990. Red's distinctive, deeply resonating bass vocals were a driving force behind the Chi-Lites great melodies. Throughout his career, Red struggled with drug dependency which seemed to spiral further out of control when the Chi-Lites were linked to charges of Federal tax evasion and fraud.

According to Mr. Thompson, he lost touch with Red when Red headed to California. However, after a local newspaper ran an article on the once prosperous entertainer, the Salvation Army and City Hall joined to establish a new humanitarian program that focused on relocating displaced homeless people.

Red Jones was one of the first homeless persons relocated to a "resettlement" apartment. This was a new beginning for Red, and it served to remove the unsightly shopping carts from the City Hall lawn.

The irony is that Creadel Jones, allowed drugs to take him down a path that piloted his life to spiral out of control when the Chi-Lites were facing FBI indictments, IRS tax evasion and fraud. Yet this homeless and destitute man, encountered politicians, lawyers, police and FBI on a daily basis as they entered and exited City Hall in Glendale, CA.

Articles written about Jones, at the time, described him

as kind, pleasant, and respectable[9]. On one occasion, Jones was asked to vacate the City Hall lawn because a memorial service was scheduled and when city officials approached Jones, he vacated without incident.

Still, the question begs to be answered… Why does Creadel "Red" Jones' family feel that Marshall Thompson of the Chi-Lites is directly responsible for the death of Jones?

In short, they have indicated that Jones was abandoned by Thompson and the Chi-Lites. Also, they have publicly stated that Thompson swindled the family out of the music and royalty rights of Creadel Jones' rightful ownership of the Chi-Lites' intellectual property. And finally, they claim that the beneficiaries of Creadel Jones' estate, namely Deborah Jones (his late wife); Darren Daniel a.k.a. Cubie; and Jones' other children, Trennell and Tammico; which he fathered while he was with the Chi-Lites and married to Deborah Jones, are due compensation. Specifically, they are referring to compensation from the rights of his music and monetary compensation (in the millions) for the royalties of remixes that were released following the death of Jones, to be recorded by Marshall Thompson, and recorded by Beyoncé and Jay-Z.

The internet is a veritable stewing cauldron of information, some good and truthful, some dishonest and deceitful. The trick is to sort through the lies, by reading between the lines, and opting for what proves to be true. How is this done? If numerous unrelated reputable sources are reporting the same facts, chances are it is somewhat trustworthy, at least to a point.

We can begin by addressing the first point: Creadel Red Jones, "… was abandoned by Marshall Thompson and the Chi-Lites." A quick internet search reveals that Jones' son, Darren, was behind this accusation. Creadel Jones' list of wives and children resemble a very long police rap sheet, and just as colorful to boot. It is no secret that the 60s and 70s was a time of awakening and expression "free love," and if you were an entertainer it is no secret that a continual stream of men and/or women would throw themselves at you.

By his own admission, son Darren confesses that he rarely ever saw his birth father (Creadel), and when he did it was nothing short of a casual social visit. Darren and his mother Deborah, made quite the scene at Harpo Studios demanding that Oprah take their side and "expose" Marshall Thompson and the Chi-Lites, but Oprah declined, and Darren and Deborah's pleas fell on deaf ears. They also attended Paternity Court TV to prove/disprove an illegitimate daughter's case when another of Jones' would-be paternal daughters attempted to stake a claim on Jones' royalties.

How was it that Creadel "Red" Jones life ended homeless and impoverished? He was asked to leave the Chi-Lites (numerous times) because of his habitual drug habit, which caused the group public embarrassment; and the Chi-Lites knew that Jones was so hooked on smack (heroin) that he was beyond reach. The Chi-Lites attempted to give Red a fresh start many times and each ended with the same results: Jones strung out and unable to perform, or impaired to the point that the group's music was affected. The final time Red and the Chi-Lites went their separate ways in 1983, Red left the Chi-Lites of his own accord and was not heard from again.

Another point to be considered is that Deborah Jones (Creadel "Red" Jones' first wife), and their son Darren, had been out of touch with Red for many years, and they did not learn of his death until three years after he perished, which is when they began their quest for Creadel "Red" Jones' royalties.

I believe we can address point two, that Thompson

"allegedly" swindled the family out of the music and royalty rights, and lastly, that Creadel Jones' beneficiaries are due compensation.

Creadel Jones died August of 1994. In 2001 Darren, Jones' son, and his mother Deborah, approached the Chi-Lites attorney, Jay B. Ross, seeking financial royalties from remakes of Chi-Lites records. Strapped for cash, Creadel's late wife approached Marshall Thompson and Brunswick Records, and she sold the rights to royalties for an undisclosed amount of cash. Deborah Jones passed in 2004, and allegedly the family was forced to give her a pauper's funeral as they did not have sufficient funds to properly bury their mother. Coincidentally, Creadel also received a pauper's funeral, as he was still homeless and destitute at the time of his passing. He was buried in an unmarked grave without even a grave marker and as he had no family or friends to provide for his eternal rest.

Therefore, if Red's wife, Deborah Jones, did in fact sell the royalty shares of his rights to Marshall Thompson, for whatever amount, then Marshall Thompson is the rightful heir of the royalties since the rights of royalty were passed on to his wife, Deborah. However, if any such document exists that can supersede the rightful legal heir under the legal court system, it has not been provided nor has it surfaced. Henceforth, it appears that Marshall Thompson is the legal owner of the royalty rights to Creadel "Red" Jones' music, and unless his living descendants (children) can provide a will or proof that Creadel left his estate and/or royalties to them, they have absolutely no chance to recoup Jones' royalties, and no legal ground to stand upon.

May he rest in peace!

**Information in this section was abstracted from Creadel "Red" Jones' son's, Darren Daniel a.k.a. Cubie's, website listed in the endnotes[10] and the appendix.

"It's a Wrap": The Conclusion

Considering the "laundry list" of indignations and transgressions that the Chi-Lites and Marshall Thompson have been exposed to over the years, it is unlikely they have been unaffected. Those who have experienced the limelight and made a career in the entertainment industry, often feel a void when not on stage.

It is typical for entertainers to sometimes view themselves in an unrealistic light because for them, the fantastic and the surreal is their reality. Everyday experiences seems to confirm that they are to be held above others in society, but with the paparazzi, the media and autograph seeking fans swarming around, it can lead to a very secluded lifestyle just to protect one's privacy. However, it is that same media and the sometimes intrusive admirers, followers, and fans that help keep them in the public eye.

As for the Chi-Lites, luck was certainly on their side in the beginning; they seemed to be destined to achieve the status of R&B and Pop music pioneers long before the band actually assembled in the late 1950's in Chicago. Each member was already a learned musician with a strong background in music. As fate would have it, the members stumbled upon one another and recognized that together they created a unique and captivating sound.

It would seem feasible to consider that if Brunswick never entered the picture, the Chi-Lites might have taken a very different path… perhaps one that would have not been clouded with charges of tax evasion, Grand Jury indictments, and connections to organized crime. If the Chi-Lites had chosen another path, and avoided Brunswick, it is possible that Red would not have become dependent on drugs after losing faith in himself, his life, and the group.

That being said, we have to also consider the alternative. If the Chi-Lites did not sign with Brunswick; if Nat Tarnapol had not been in charge of their destination; if Tommy Vastola was not involved in the shaping of the Chi-Lites, there remains the possibility that they would never have left the practice sessions on the street corner of Chicago's south side; and the world would have been cheated out of one of the most influential vocal groups in history.

The influence the Chi-Lites had on history with the Black Panther and "Power to the People" movement, and the designation of Chicago as "Chi-Town," is a testament to the courage the Chi-Lites exemplified, and the love they had for their birthplace. The perfect amalgam creating the finest pedigree in Pop music advanced and changed music theory with unsophisticated methods and innovative harmonies. Despite negative influence from the entertainment industry, and the corrupt world of organized crime, the Chi-Lites outlasted many other entertainers.

The fact that many artists have recovered the Chi-Lites songs speaks to the influence, power, and sustainability of the Chi-Lites. The chart-busting, Chi-Lites hit, "Have You Seen Her," written by Eugene Record and Barbara Acklin was re-released in 1990 by MC Hammer on his Gold album, *Please Hammer Don't Hurt 'Em*.

The next big hit for the Chi-Lites, "Oh Girl," released in 1972, also written by Eugene Record, became a Billboard Top 100 number one single in May of 1972. It was re-released by the British Hip-Hop artist, Hard Livin'; and Leo Sayer re-released it on his album, *Here*. Country music artist; Con Hunley took it to number 12 on the Billboard Hot Country Singles Chart in 1982. Additionally, Adult Contemporary artist, Paul Young's rendition of the song soared to the top of the charts in 1990. Further recordings include: punk band, Me First, and the Gimme Gimmes in 2003; southern rapper Paul Wall in 2006; and Seal in 2011.

In 1989, UB40 put their own personal impression on the Chi-Lites' hit record, "Homely Girl." In 2012, *The Jam* reissued, "Stoned Out of My Mind." And more recently and notably, Beyoncé and Jay-Z sang a duet to the musical track of "Are You My Woman (Tell Me So)," and over dubbed the vocal track to produce one of their greatest songs, "Crazy In Love." Gospel recording artist, BeBe Winans altered the words to "Have You Seen Her," and changed the title to, "Do You Know Him[11]."

Perhaps the most entertaining was to hear television's character, Tony Soprano in the season four episode of the Sopranos entitled, *Watching Too Much Television*, in 2002. Tony is in the locker room of his athletic club when "Oh Girl" begins to play on the radio. Another man in the locker room says, "I love this song." Tony retorts, "Chi-Lites. The best!" The other man says, "Believe it or not the Chi-Lites were signed to the same label as Tommy James and them damn Shondells." Then Tony Soprano sets him straight, "See a lot of people think that, but they're wrong... Chi-Lites were on Brunswick." The song plays on for about 10 seconds, and Tony stares off and smiles.

The scene shifts to Tony in a confrontation with one of his friends who is currently in a relationship with Tony's ex-girlfriend. Next it shifts to Tony driving in the car (a night scene). "Oh Girl" begins playing on the radio, and Tony Soprano sings along. Here we see the penetrating power that the Chi-Lites music has on the heart, even a tough-as-nails mobster, who wouldn't blink an eye at ending the life of (as he says) a scumbag double-crosser. He begins to sob like a baby as he joins the Chi-Lites in singing, "Oh Girl." The song continues as Tony drives to his friend's home, begins to beat him with a belt and says, "All the girls in New Jersey and you had to fuck this one." Then the music fades as the screen dims.

Marshall Thompson of the Chi-Lites is an accomplished performer who many musicians and entertainers desire to emulate, especially when you consider he had the endurance to last more than five decades. A major inspiration in history, confronting issues of social inequity through activism and harmony, and a tribute to the music industry, the Chi-Lites defied the odds and overcame the obstacles placed before them. The Chi-Lites fantastical career clearly stands as a declaration that dreams do come true.

Millions of bands try to make their mark in the music industry, and tens-of-thousands of bands release "one-hit wonders," and never progress any further. It is not often that the key elements come together in a way that the main players in the group sync in unison well enough to project the entire package. In the case of the Chi-Lites, as you have read their impact on history and society has achieved such adoration and devotion that it has implored us to look past the moral indignations and accusation that would have otherwise ended, or at least, stained an entertainer's career.

From activities involving the Black Panthers, to defrauding the IRS out of taxes, and mixing with the likes of organized crime figures, to incarceration for his role in illegally selling badges for personal gain, the Chi-Lites and Marshall Thompson managed somehow to survive the storms and find the sunshine. Stricken with a life-altering stroke, Marshall Thompson has proven to be the Chi-Lites' "Last Man Standing."

Inspirational Messages from Friends and Supporters of the Chi-Lites

"Back in the day, as a Chicago On Air Radio Personality, I was excited every time the Chi-Lites released a new single or LP because I knew it would be a hit and that concerts would be sold out. Fifty plus years later, I still see the same excitement from fans, and I still feel the same excitement myself when I listen to their music.

If ever there were a rags to riches story, it is Marshall Thompson, the leader of the Chi-Lites. I have never known a singer so determined to succeed. Marshall was never shy about promoting The Chi-Lites and it is a known fact that he is a promotional genius, filled with energy and enthusiasm. The stage costumes were amazing, and truly represented the Chi-Lites. With all this said, and based on the Chi-Lites fifty plus years of success, this book is destined to become a best seller."

Herb Kent ~ Radio DJ: Inducted into Radio Hall of Fame 1995 - In 2009, the Guinness World Records certified Herb Kent as the longest tenured deejay, having at that time spent 66 years on the airwaves in Chicago (that time currently is 71 years on the airwaves as an active radio DJ).[12]

"The Chi-Lites were one of my favorite groups. I especially liked the song, 'Hot on a Thing,' and still haven't tired of it because of that unique beat and instrumentation. I have a special segment on my show called *Back Street Memories*, and I still play the Chi-Lites. I've also interviewed dozens of groups from that era such as the Dells, Flamingos, Dixie Cups, Bobby Vee, Bobby Rydell, and Archie Drell to name a few, but I've never had the pleasure of interviewing the Chi-Lites. I would love to add Marshall to that list of memorable list of interviewees."

DJ Chuck Stevens of Rock-N-Roll Syndications

◊

"The Chi-Lites done the job! Straight after the Revue releases they were signed by Brunswick, and the rest is history. We have been the best of friends talking daily, ever since. My best to you on your book, Marshall. Your legacy endures!"

Garland Green ~ Soul Singer and Pianist

"Marshall, congratulations from the Jubilee Travelers on your new book. Best of luck and best wishes. Thank you, Minister Seamore"
Jubilee Travelers

"Marshall Thompson is a lifelong childhood friend, whom I met in the drum and bugle corps in Chicago's Ida B. Wells projects at the age of 14. We lost track of one another for a short period, but our paths crossed again shortly after at the age of 18 at the Regal Theatre in Chicago. Marshall was performing as drummer for Major Lance, another mutual childhood friend.

Surprisingly, we met up once again at Carl Davis's office. My dear friend, Otis Leavell, brought Marshall to meet Carl Davis so that they could help start a male R&B/Soul Group – The Chi-Lites. Since then, we became best friends and worked together on The Chi-Lites first two smash hits, 'Have You Seen Her,' and 'Oh Girl.'

I served as The Chi-Lites tour manager for 'The Super

Soul Spectacular Tour,' which was produced by Carl Davis, Gene Chandler, and myself. This was Marshall's first major concert tour and helped break him and the Chi-Lites in as major artists. Marshall was also one of the first artists from Chicago to help launch, 'Soul Train' with Don Cornelius; he and the Chi-Lites performed in their pilot episodes. Amongst many of Marshall's closest friends and fans, he has been designated as the 'Godfather of Male R&B Soul Groups.' Marshall Thompson is a true legend!"

Gus Redmond – Musician/Songwriter /Producer/Executive

"When you think of where soulful records come from

you might think of Memphis or Philadelphia... but then there were the Chi-Lites from Chicago. I've been playing records on the radio since 1974, and the Chi-Lites were always a staple. Eugene Records co-wrote the single, 'Have You Seen Her.' It became a million seller and still gets played today. Eugene performed the song on *SNL* (Saturday Night Live) in 1978. MC (MC Hammer) would 'cover' the song in 1990, and the song became a hit all over again. Eugene died in 2005 after a long battle with cancer. He was 64."

Bart Shore radio DJ – WBBM News Radio & Time Warp Radio

◊

"I will never forget the first time I heard the song, 'Oh Girl' on the radio. It just seemed to jump out like no other record. From the opening melodica (harmonic keyboard) to Eugene Record's amazing voice, it was clear this was destined to be a special song. Eugene captured the emotion of the story so perfectly, you couldn't help but experience every word of the lyrics on a personal level."

Greg Brown – WLS (Midday host on 94.7 WLS Radio)

◊

"Congratulations Marshall… on your overdue book. We, the Classic Sullivans are proud of you. Eddie, Lorraine, and our beloved sister, Barbara."

Eddie Sullivan (the Classic Sullivans)

◊

"Marshall and I go back more than 40 years...back to the days when I was a disc jockey at WGRT in Chicago. Eddie Morrison was the Program Director, and the Chi-Lites had a hit record called, 'Have You Seen Her' followed by the smash hit, 'Oh Girl.' Not only was Marshall a phenomenal entertainer, but his enthusiasm would have made him one of the best record promotion men in the business if that had been his career choice. Marshall chose to share his talent as a performer on the stages of the world, with the hit-making recording artists known as the Chi-Lites. With his 100-watt smile, musical gifts, and his knowledge of show business, it's easy to see why Marshall is the Last Man Standing. He's the only original Chi-lite with the group, but he makes sure the news guys are at the top of their game both musically and visually. Their on-stage performances are flawless, and they are always impeccably dressed. Kudos and credit to the *Last Man Standing* ...my friend Marshall Thompson."

Richard Steele ~ Radio DJ and award winning host and correspondent on Chicago's 91.5 WBEZ Radio.

"I remember when the Chi-Lites came to Saginaw, MI. I was 16 years old and it was the first time I saw them perform. I was blown away by their sound and showmanship; they sang in perfect harmony and danced with style and precision. The Chi Lites have definitely put their mark on the Music industry. To the fellas; Eugene Record, Creadel "Red" Jones, Robert "Squirrel" Lester, and Marshall Thompson, I would just like to say, 'Job Well Done.' And to Marshall, the last man standing, I would like to say to you, 'a winner never quits, and a quitter never wins.' And you're a winner!"

Larry "L.J." Reynolds - of the Dramatics

◊

"Marshall is truly one of the hardest working men in show business, and taught me a lot in the short time I have been with the Chi-Lites. He really has been a great mentor to me. In our travels around the world, I have seen first-hand how much he is respected in the industry. Marshall is a great entertainer and an even greater friend."

Fred Simon - Lost Generation (Sly, Slick and Wicked), current vocalist with the Chi-Lites.

◊

"I met the Chi-Lites backstage while working in radio in Hartford, CT., back in April 1973. I could tell right away they were very cool, likeable guys. They played at Bushnell Memorial Concert and they played my favorite song, '(For God Sake) Give More Power to the People.' The introduction for that song was fairly long with an amazing build-up, and an enthusiastic crowd. A DJ delights to talk up the vocal. It was a memorable event with a great bunch of talented guys."

Gnarly Charlie - (currently) South Florida. 1980's DJ

◊

"Our relationship began through radio legend, Herb Kent many years ago and we have been friends ever since. I just want to say that Marshall Thompson is one of the kindest and most giving persons in all of show business. After the passing of my late wife Anaia, to breast cancer in April of 2004, Marshall often donated his time, talent and money to helping me to make women of color, aware of the importance of getting mammogram screenings, for the early detection of the disease. He has also helped tremendously in our annual Christmas Food Drive for disadvantaged families on Chicago's south side."

Ken Bedford ~ Entertainer, Radio DJ, and MC

"Marshall Thompson is the man with the magnetic personality. He always had a super strong drive to succeed and through the ups and downs, he did what it took to succeed whether he had to crawl, walk, or run. He kicked doors open (figuratively) to make things happen for the Chi Lites and other artists. It's been over five decades of fame. Keep up the good work, Marshall!"

Clifford Curry and The Notations

◊

"I'm very proud of you and your career accomplishments over the years. I look forward to 40 more years of friendship with you my brother! Respect 4 Life!"

Walter "Breezy" Chism Jr. ~Program Director/ On Air Host: The Breezy Radio Show - Live365.com/ KHDBRadio.com

◊

"In 1998, a well-dressed man approached me, and asked, "… have you ever done any bodyguard work?" I replied, "Yes, why do you ask?"

I did not know whom I was talking to, until he told me he was Marshall Thompson of The Chi-Lites. He explained that he needed a female guard to work with him in Vegas. So, off to Vegas we went. Little did I know, my duty was to guard 48 men and 4 females for the 70's Soul Jam Tour.

The next morning 'Boss Man' (a.k.a. Marshall) called me to the back of the bus and handed me a paper. I looked at the paper and it was an application for employment as Head of Security for The Chi-Lites. Marshall said, I like the way you handle business and you will be out here for 6 weeks, starting now, if you want the job. I've been with Marshall for over 10 years.

From my perspective Marshall is the best boss to

work for; he is caring, funny, loving, and a wonderful person. I love Marshall Thompson, my friend, and my 'Boss Man.'"

Gloria J. Adams ~ Head of Security: Chi-Lites

"I have been fortunate enough to be part of the legacy of the Chi-Lites by working as Marshall Thompson's personal videographer. Working for Marshall always makes you feel like you're filming or producing something that people will see forever, all over the world, long after we are gone.

Working for a man that I consider to be one of the hardest working people in show business has taught me valuable lessons on how to be successful and go after your dreams. He is indeed a true ican and a legend.

Marshall thank you for letting me be a part of your life."

Last Man Standing

Erik Hammond

~Erik Hammond~Independent Film Producer:
Clear Vision Multimedia Video & Film Production Inc.

"Dear Uncle Marshall, I know this has been a long process, driven by your passion for music and song writing. You have given me a vision of production that can't be taught in any school. Thank you for giving me away on my special (wedding) day; what more could a girl ask for? You have been a huge supporter of the Dream Castle Villa in Montego Bay Jamaica, and I am grateful and thankful for you."

We love you & Congratulations on your book!
Gwen (Nicks) & Michael
◊

"As a kid growing up on the Southside of Chicago, I was naturally a big fan of the Chicago soul sound; and Marshall Thompson and the Chi-Lites were both literally and figuratively instrumental in defining the genre. Their hits, 'Have You Seen Her' and 'Oh Girl,' are as classic today as they were when I first heard them as a kid—we can all learn from Marshall's career and the contributions he and the band made to Chicago culture."
John W. Rogers Jr. ~ Chairman & Chief Executive Officer of Ariel Investments"
◊

"Marshall Thompson is one of the nicest individuals that I know. He is engaging, warm and very likeable. Marshall and I have even spent time reading the Bible together, and we both realize the importance of a relationship with God.

I remember when I was a kid, I was a huge follower of many great songs by The Chi-Lites such as 'Have You Seen Her,' 'Oh Girl,' 'A Letter to Myself,' and one of my all-time favorites, 'Hot On A Thing.' I am delighted to say that Marshall's positive attitude brings a smile to many faces in many parts of America and this world."
Elroy Smith ~ Radio Programmer
◊

"I met Marshall Thompson and the Chi-Lites for the first time back in the 1980s when they performed in a show that also featured the Stylistics at Maywood Park Race Track in Illinois. The first thing that impressed me about the group was their precision to detail involving wardrobe, music, and the entire presentation. I had the pleasure of working with them on numerous occasions, and they were

always striving for perfection and checking the integrity of the music and the look of the group. These likeable and talented guys have managed to foster a legacy of timeless and 'real' music. The Chi-Lites always give their best."
Ron Onesti-President and CEO of Onesti Entertainment and Arcada Theater, St. Charles, IL

◊

It is with great pride that support my friend, the talented Mr. Marshall Thompson, of The Chi-Lites. I am honored to be the Chi-Lites Oklahoma City connection at KTLR 94.1 FM. As pioneers, and having more than 50 Years on radio and in the broadcasting industry, Marshall and I share the magnificent class of few who have become living legends – and a glorious position to share!

I am promoting "The Last Man Standing" as the Chi-Lites music paved the way for a new breed of musicians and Marshall Thompson's work ethic is the very finest in the music industry. I am truly honored to have had the opportunity to work with the Chi-Lites and Marshall over the years. Marshall Thompson has always supported me and I him, he truly is the… "Last Man Standing!"

It's A Windy City Affair
Charles Hightower ' Program Director
One Accord Broadcasting Corp/KTLR 94.1 FM

Biographical and Historic Information

Dane Ladwig

Dane Ladwig is a native of Chicago. Dane has passionately pursued his vision of writing. The vivid imagery demonstrated in his wiring reflects his love for Chicago and its residents, particularly the downtrodden and less fortunate. He admires and admonishes those who defy the odds and stand out as examples in their communities.

Dane has a natural talent for capturing the essence of humanity at its very core. As a budding journalist straight out of college, Dane felt more compelled to write about matters that tugged at his heart and as he put it, "People are the real deal. When I can preserve the rich history and culture of a society by composing sentences and paragraphs, to me, I have accomplished something very special… that, to me, is a triumphant and victorious endeavor."

When not composing his next masterpiece, Dane Ladwig says, "I really enjoy listening to music. I actually like to listen to my old 45's and LP's on an old Zenith turntable that I've had since I was a kid. MP3's and computerization is nice, don't get me wrong, but that's the way they were intended to be heard, mono (as opposed to stereo), scratches and all. That's what gets me going."

"Dane Ladwig has been recognized and accredited by the General Assembly for his writing accomplishments. He is listed in the top 100 authors on AuthorsDB, and he has been included to and registered on the International Best Sellers list.

Current Members

Marshall Thompson - 1959-2001, 2002-present (born August 24, 1942, Chicago)
Tara Henderson - 2001-present (born Chicago)
Fred Simon - 2010-present (born Chicago)

Former Members

Robert Squirrel Lester - 1959-2010 (born August 16, 1942, McComb, Mississippi; died January 21, 2010, Chicago)
Eugene Record - 1959-1973, 1980-1988 (born December 23, 1940, Chicago; died July 22, 2005[2])
Creadel "Red" Jones - 1959-1973, 1980-1982 (born September 26, 1940, Chicago; died August 25, 1994)
Clarence Johnson - 1959-1964
Stanley Anderson - 1973
Willie Kensey - 1973
Doc Roberson - 1973
David Scott - 1973-1980
Danny Johnson - 1973-1977
Vandy Hampton - 1977-1980
Frank Reed - 1988, 1990-1993, 1996-1998, 2001-2014 (born September 16, 1954, Omaha, Nebraska; died February 26, 2014)[1]
Anthony Watson - 1988-1990, 1993-1996, 1998-2002 (born Mobile, Alabama)

Chi-Lites Discography

Studio Albums

Year	Album
1969	Give It Away
1970	I Like Your Lovin' (Do You Like Mine?)
1971	(For God's Sake) Give More Power to the People
1972	A Lonely Man
1973	A Letter to Myself
	Chi-Lites
1974	Toby
1975	Half a Love
1976	Happy Being Lonely
1977	The Fantastic Chi-Lites
1980	Heavenly Body
1981	Love Your Way Through
1982	Me and You
1983	Bottom's Up
1984	Steppin' Out
1990	Just Say You Love Me
1998	Help Wanted
2006	Low Key

Compilation Albums

Year	Album
1972	Greatest Hits
1976	Greatest Hits, Vol. 2
1983	Greatest Hits
1992	Greatest Hits

Year	Title
1996	Inner City Blues
	Greatest Hits, Vol. 2
1998	Too Good to Be Forgotten
	Remembered
	Hit Highlights from The Chi-Lites
1999	Have You Seen Her: Their Greatest Hits
2001	20 Greatest Hits
2002	The Best of The Chi-Lites
	Have You Seen Her
2003	The Best of The Chi-Lites
2006	The Ultimate Chi-Lites

SINGLES

Year	Title
1964	"You Did That to Me" (credited as The Hi-Lites)
1965	"I'm So Jealous"
	"Ain't You Glad (Winter's Over)"
	"Never No More"
1966	"Pretty Girl" (credited as Mashall & The Chi-Lites)
1967	"Price of Love" (credited as Mashall & The Chi-Lites)
	"Love Me"
1968	"(Um, Um) My Baby Loves Me"
1969	"Give It Away"
	"Let Me Be the Man My Daddy Was" (A-side)
	"The Twelfth of Never" (B-side)
	"To Change My Love"

1970	"24 Hours of Sadness"
	"I Like Your Lovin' (Do You Like Mine)"
	"Are You My Woman? (Tell Me So)"
1971	"(For God's Sake) Give More Power to the People"
	"We Are Neighbors"
	"I Want to Pay You Back (For Loving Me)"
	"Have You Seen Her"
1972	"Oh Girl"
	"The Coldest Days of My Life (Part 1)"
	"A Lonely Man" (A-side)
	"The Man & the Woman (The Boy & the Girl)" (B-side)
	"We Need Order"
1973	"A Letter to Myself"
	"My Heart Just Keeps on Breakin'"
	"Stoned Out of My Mind"
	"I Found Sunshine"
1974	"Homely Girl"
	"I Forgot to Say I Love You Till I'm Gone"
	"There Will Never Be Any Peace (Until God Is Seated at the Conference Table)"
	"You Got to Be the One"
	"Too Good to Be Forgotten"
	"Toby" (A-side)
	"That's How Long" (B-side)
1975	"Have You Seen Her" / "Oh Girl" (re-release)
	"It's Time for Love" (A-side)
	"Here I Am" (B-side)
	"Don't Burn No Bridges" (with Jackie Wilson)

1976	"The Devil Is Doing His Work"
	"You Don't Have to Go"
	"Happy Being Lonely"
1977	"Vanishing Love" (A-side)
	"I Turn Away" (B-side)
	"My First Mistake"
	"If I Had a Girl"
1978	"The First Time (Ever I Saw Your Face)"
1979	"Higher"
1980	"The Only One for Me (One in a Million)"
	"Heavenly Body"
1981	"Have You Seen Her" (re-recorded version)
	"All I Wanna Do Is Make Love to You"
	"Me and You"
1982	"Hot on a Thing (Called Love)"
	"Try My Side (Of Love)"
1983	"Bottom's Up"
	"Bad Motor Scooter"
	"Have You Seen Her" (re-release)
	"Changing for You"
1984	"Stop What You're Doin'"
	"Gimme Whatcha Got"
1985	"Hard Act to Follow"
1990	"There's a Change"
1997	"Help Wanted (Heroes Are in Short Supply)"
1998	"Hold on to Your Dreams"

Discography chart: Wikipedia.com

Appendix

Links to Darren (Cubie) Jones articles:

- http://en.wikipedia.org/wiki/Glendale,_California
- http://articles.latimes.com/1990-05-31/news/gl-763_1_city-hall
- http://www.absoluteastronomy.com/discussionpost/Whats_Being_Denied__From_The_Record_Company_Chi_Lites___72876
- http://www.entertainersagainstcorruptionmagazine.com/chi-lites-son.php
- http://www.topix.com/forum/who/the-chi-lites/TBKAPQDI9V07FEAQ4
- http://www.topix.com/forum/who/the-chi-lites/TRSDV3CIPUFD38364
- http://www.topix.com/forum/who/oprah-winfrey/TNFICC15MPEURVGJE
- http://www.charliegillett.com/bb/viewtopic.php?f=10&t=990

End Notes

1. http://www.history-of-rock.com/freed.htm
2. http://en.wikipedia.org/wiki/Racketeer_Influenced_and_Corrupt_Organizations_Act
3. http://en.wikipedia.org/wiki/Jackie_Wilson
4. http://en.wikipedia.org/wiki/Jackie_Wilson
5. http://jackiewilsonlover.wordpress.com/2012/08/02tommy-jamess-memoir/
6. http://jackiewilsonlover.wordpress.com/page/7/
7. http://en.wikipedia.org/wiki/Death_of_John_Lennon
8. http://www.nytimes.com/1992/07/15/nyregion/4-indicted-in-plot-to-kill-informer.html
9. http://articles.latimes.com/1990-05-31/news/gl-763_1_city-hall
10. http://www.entertainersagainstcorruptionmagazine.com/news.php
11. Jet Magazine. In The Spotlight, page 40. Singer-Songwriter/Producer Eugene Record of Chi-Lites Fame Adds Spice to Beyoncé Hit. October 20, 2003
12. http://radio.about.com/od/legendarydjs/p/Radio-Profile-Herb-Kent.htm

©2014
Anytime Enterprises, LLC.

CPSIA information can be obtained
at www.ICGtesting.com
Printed in the USA
FSHW021305051118
53561FS